Publishing

Publishing

A WRITER'S MEMOIR

GAIL GODWIN

ILLUSTRATIONS BY FRANCES HALSBAND

B L O O M S B U R Y

NEW YORK · LONDON · OXFORD · NEW DELHI · SYDNEY

IN MEMORY OF THE FIRST GIRL WHO WROTE

KATHLEEN KRAHENBUHL GODWIN COLE

Bloomsbury USA
An imprint of Bloomsbury Publishing Plc

1385 Broadway	50 Bedford Square
New York	London
NY 10018	WC1B 3DP
USA	UK

www.bloomsbury.com

BLOOMSBURY and the Diana logo are trademarks of Bloomsbury Publishing Plc

First published 2015
This paperback edition published 2016

Text © Gail Godwin, 2015
Illustrations © Frances Halsband, 2015

ISBN: HB: 978-1-62040-824-7
ePub: 978-1-62040-826-1
PB: 978-1-62040-825-4

Library of Congress Cataloging-in-Publication Data
Godwin, Gail.
Publishing : a Writer's Memoir / Gail Godwin; illustrations
by Frances Halsband. —First U.S. Edition.
pages cm
ISBN 978-1-62040-824-7 (hardback)
1. Godwin, Gail. 2. Women authors, American—20th century—
Biography. 3. Publishers and publishing—United States—Biography.
4. Authorship. I. Halsband, Frances, illustrator. II. Title.
PS3557.O315Z46 2015
813'.54—dc23
[B]
2014014696

2 4 6 8 10 9 7 5 3 1

Typeset by Hewer Text UK Ltd, Edinburgh
Printed and bound in USA by Berryville Graphics Inc., Berryville, Virginia

To find out more about our authors and books visit www.bloomsbury.com. Here you will find extracts,
author interviews, details of forthcoming events, and the option to sign up for our newsletters.

Bloomsbury books may be purchased for business or promotional use. For information on bulk purchases
please contact Macmillan Corporate and Premium Sales Department at specialmarkets@macmillan.com.

Louis Round Wilson Library, formerly the university library, now
the home of the Southern Collection and Gail Godwin's archives.

Publishing

CONTENTS

Foreword

This little volume is a meditation on publishing—on the hunger to be published, on the pursuit of publication, and on the practices and preoccupations that go with being a published writer.

In no way does it claim to be even a very small slice of the history of American publishing in my lifetime. It is more of an offering, with variations composed around a single theme, like Bach's *The Musical Offering*.

Its viewpoint is personal, written by a former little girl who watched her mother type stories straight out of her head and then walked with that mother to the mailbox to gather envelopes with checks inside from a New York literary agent.

Publishing is about wanting for a long time to be a published writer and about the condition of living as a writer for a long time after you are published.

Publishing Hunger

THE GIRLS WHO WROTE

The university was a charming, an unforgettable place. It was situated in the little village of Pulpit Hill, in the central midland of the big state. Students came and departed by motor from the dreary tobacco town of Exeter, twelve miles away: the countryside was raw, powerful and ugly, a rolling land of field, wood, and hollow; but the university itself was buried in a pastoral wilderness, on a long tabling butte, which rose steeply above the country. One burst suddenly, at the hill-top, on the end of the straggling village street, flanked by faculty houses, and winding a mile in to the town centre and the university. The central campus sloped back and up over an area of rich turf, groved with magnificent ancient trees. A quadrangle of post-Revolutionary buildings of weathered brick bounded the upper end: other new buildings, in the modern bad manner (the pedagogic Neo-Greeky), were scattered around beyond the central design: beyond, there was a thickly forested wilderness. . . . It seemed to Eugene like a

*provincial outpost of great Rome: the wilderness crept up
to it like a beast.*

Thomas Wolfe, *Look Homeward, Angel* (1929)

CHAPEL HILL, 1958

Each spring Alfred A. Knopf, the distinguished publisher of
Willa Cather, Albert Camus, Isak Dinesen, André Gide, and
Thomas Mann, sent New York scouts to the campus in
search of new talent. Students with manuscripts in progress
were invited to present themselves at a specified classroom
in the English building. When your turn came with the
scout, you would hand over your five typewritten pages of
the work—*not* a synopsis or description of what the work
was going to be—and wait beside the scout while those
pages were read.

My novel in progress, *Windy Peaks*, was going to be about
the staff and summer guests at a resort hotel on the highest
peak in the state. I thought of it as my potential *Magic
Mountain*, which I had not read yet, but I would not court
ridicule by suggesting this comparison to anybody, or even
by hinting at such in a synopsis—which anyway wasn't
allowed by the Knopf scouts. My five pages were given over
to a single character, which was a shame, considering how

many people were going to be important in the book, but I had to start somewhere and I liked the idea of an intriguing young man on the make hitchhiking up the mountain *at night* to his summer job at Windy Peaks Manor. Though only a lowly busboy, he would insert his way into the lives of all the characters, high and low, male and female, before the summer's end. His ambitious brain was teeming with plots and plans to make himself the leading man in his story as he stood in the dark in the thin air of that mountain road waiting for the next beam of headlights. Actually, though I hadn't heard of that novel yet, he was more like the protagonist of *Confessions of Felix Krull, Confidence Man*, which Thomas Mann wrote in a burst of playfulness when he was seventy-nine.

The scouts this year were a couple. A middle-aged man wearing an ascot greeted me and told me to take a seat at any desk. I had taken a course in modern fiction (intensive readings of *To the Lighthouse* followed by *A Portrait of the Artist as a Young Man*) in this same second-floor room of Bingham Hall, looking out at Wilson Library and the quad enclosed by the old oaks and "Neo-Greeky" buildings already described by the Great American Novelist from my hometown.

His wife, the man informed me, was behind that folding screen which had been placed in front of the teacher's desk, "so you will have your privacy with her." He wrote my name on a clipboard and said I would be called. I plopped down in a swirl of self-conscious misgivings, unable to notice anything. Other names were called and students shuffled forward, disappeared behind the screen, and then shuffled out another door. By the time my turn came to go behind the screen, my own name sounded as nonsensical as the book title I had typed in boldface on my manila folder.

The wife-scout sat erect as a martinet in the same swivel chair in which my former professor had swayed and slouched, his cigarette ash lengthening dangerously above his necktie, as he alerted us to the many ways James Joyce was going to employ the words *cold*, *wet*, and *damp* for mood effects. The scout was a chic, formidable number, a little too old for the hair color to be all her own. After she had finished writing something in a notebook, she looked up as if bringing me into existence and asked if I would mind standing on her left while she read my work. "No, ma'am, of course not," I said, wondering if there was anything sinister about her specifying the left side.

The scout's manicured fingers (polished with a sophisticated shade of brownish mauve) were actually touching my pages. She wore an emerald wedding ring in an old-fashioned setting. On the second page she uttered a little *hmpf* of surprise and I was dying to ask "what?" but was afraid of jinxing the proceedings. At last, she sat up even straighter, clacked the pages together, replaced them in the folder, and handed it back to me with a crisp sketch of a smile. "Sorry, this isn't right for us," she said, "but good luck." She was writing something in the notebook as the already invisible author of *Windy Peaks* shuffled out.

I headed up the quad, back to gloomy, echoing Bynum Hall, where I was majoring in journalism. Bynum, which had been the men's basketball gymnasium until they got a better one, was directly adjacent to the sunny Greek Revival temple that housed the Playmakers Theater, where my mother as a graduate student had written, directed, designed, and acted in her own plays. As I slogged along inside my bubble of failure beneath the Great American Novelist's ancient trees, it struck me for the first time that I was nothing new, just the latest model of a young person hungry for success, and possibly one of the very many who was not going to make it. I walked in my mother's own footsteps, until she would have turned left toward the Playmakers' sunny temple, and continued on alone to gloomy Bynum.

Twenty-four years earlier she had trod these paths, from library to English building to the Playmakers Theater. Her master's thesis had been on Inigo Jones's influence on Ben

Looking toward Bynum from the porch of Playmakers Theater
"I walked in my mother's own footsteps, until she would
have turned left toward the Playmakers sunny temple,
and continued on alone to gloomy Bynum."

Jonson's masques. If I had known where to look in the Playmakers' scene shop, I probably could have unearthed some of Kathleen Krahenbuhl's old props. ("I was always very particular with my props. Proff Koch said he admired my attention to details. He always insisted on being called Proff, with two *ff*'s. If someone in a play I wrote had painted a picture, I painted that picture and framed it and hung it on the wall of my set.")

My mother and I told each other stories as soon as I could form a sentence. She told me about her triumphs at Chapel Hill, her plays, her professors, her boyfriends. Those were her happy years. Two years later, she would be sitting on her parents' porch when a handsome man with a broken ankle swung by on crutches and her dog ran out and bit him. Within a few months she had married him, already knowing it wouldn't last.

We made up stories together, in which I was allowed to do awful things under the alias of someone called Theophilus, the Awfullest Bear in the World. We took turns "reading" stories out of a tiny address book with blank pages. We also drew pictures and acted scenes based on real people from church and school, also cousins and the people who worked with my mother on the newspaper. One of us would draw a person or walk across the room in a certain way and the other would have to guess who it was.

It became comfortable for me to cast my life, her life, into the mold of a story. The first full-length story I ever wrote, at nine, was about me in the disguise of a henpecked husband, one Ollie McGonnigle. His "wife" was my grandmother and mother in their disciplinary modes, and the Mayor of the Town, who keeps Ollie in his place, was our cousin Bill, from across the street, the authority who was cited when they needed male backup. (Bill really was the mayor of Weaverville.)

When my mother started selling love stories to the pulp magazines, I was old enough to begin to guess at the unacceptable or sad parts of the girls' lives she'd had to leave out in order to get published. In my teens, we sometimes wrote the same story from different angles. We would assign ourselves a premise and setting, like "The Magic Lipstick," and tell it from our separate points of view. Her "Magic Lipstick" narrator was "an older woman in her thirties" at a dance who befriends a young girl crying in the powder room. Nobody has asked the girl to dance. The woman takes a lipstick from her purse and says it has the power to bestow confidence and appeal. She gives it to the girl and, after a reassuring talk that does the real bestowing work, returns to her husband's table. When the husband presently comments on "that girl who looks so happy being whirled around the floor," the wife murmurs wisely, "Yes, it's wonderful what a little confidence will do." My "Magic Lipstick," from the unhappy girl's point of view, dwelt lovingly and lengthily on the inner aspects of feeling unpopular and then tacked on the unconvincing ending of her triumphal return to the dance floor wearing the magic lipstick. I got more satisfaction rereading my mother's story, but I also admired some of my brooding insights about the state of being rejected.

One of my plays for Proff was about two girls who go to New York. I called it *Manhattan Twilight* in production, though it had another title first. The first girl, Jean—who I played—wanted to be a writer. Her friend Ann—played by my friend Ruth—wanted to be an artist. Well, I decided the set ought to at least have one painting by Ann hanging on the wall of their apartment, so I looked through art books till I found the kind of landscape Ann would paint and then I painted it. Proff said it looked very professional. I told him it was easy to copy something after someone else had come up with the original idea. The apartment in my play also needed a window and I found a blown-up photograph of a New York skyline and tinted it with a deep blue wash and cut it to fit the window. It really did look like they had that view outside their window.

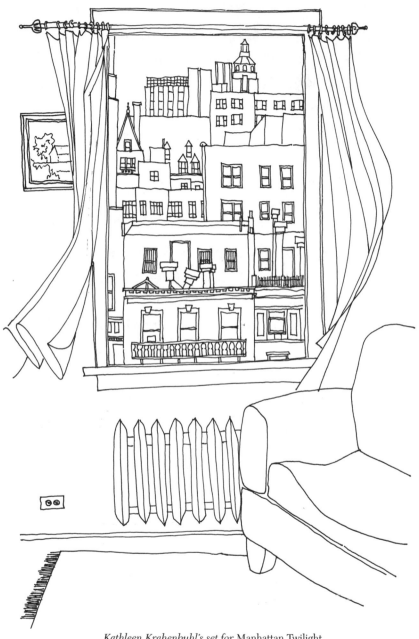

Kathleen Krahenbuhl's set for Manhattan Twilight

"Proff said it looked very professional."

Many years later, when I was going through my mother's papers following her death at age seventy-seven in a car crash, I came across the yellowed typescript of a one-act play called *Borrowed of the Night: A Tragedy of Youth*, by Kathleen Krahenbuhl. It was dated 1934. As soon as I saw the synopsis, I realized I was holding *Manhattan Twilight* in my hands. There was a foreword—she had typed "Foreward," then penciled in an *o* over her mistake. The twenty-two-year-old voice of this foreword was respectful, candid, and disarmingly modest. It was probably addressed to "Proff Koch" and the members of her playwriting class.

I don't know exactly when I thought of the idea for this play but I have had it for a long time and once attempted to write a short story on it. I was thinking of lighting effects and decided it would be a very nice place to use a blue light, for example, a blue spot following Ann when she thinks she is blind. So I decided to try to make it into a play.

None of the characters are real people though they are naturally based on people I know. I used Mrs. McGinnis merely as someone who could further the plot by letting people know something of the background of the story in her conversation with Jean. In a short story this could be done merely by telling the thoughts of Jean but solilo-quies are too hard to write and unless they are very good are not effective so I thought I had better make a dialogue between two characters, one being Jean and the other the most probable person who might come in and have a good reason to come.

A synopsis followed:

After years of work and study Ann has become a successful illustrator but she wants to go abroad to study so that she may paint something really good. Jean who is a reporter and tries to write short stories that just do not sell shares an apartment with Ann in the house of Mrs. McGinnis.

When the play opens Mrs. McGinnis and Jean are discussing Ann's great talent and how hard she works and her bad habit of working into the twilight without turning on any lights. Mrs. McGinnis leaves and Ann comes home very dejected. She tells Jean she has seen an eye specialist who says she may be going to lose her eyesight but he can't tell her how much time she has left. Jean comforts her and says they are going to consult other specialists and urges Ann not to give up. Then Jean leaves to go to work and Ann begins to draw in the fading light. Suddenly the stage goes dark. Ann thinks her blindness has come, decides there is nothing left to live for, and jumps out the window. Then the lights go on as Mrs. McGinnis returns to tell Ann there has been a brief blackout over the whole city. But she speaks to an empty room.

The ending of the synopsis came as a shock. Had I simply forgotten the ending, or had my mother always left it out in her tellings? But what really gave me a pang was that part about Jean trying to write short stories "that just do not sell." Could it be that, already as a student, my mother had been sending out stories and getting them rejected? If so, what kinds of stories were they? Her love stories written in her spare time during her wartime stint as a reporter on the *Asheville Citizen-Times* had been hugely successful; sometimes two of them appeared in the same issue of a magazine, one under Kathleen Godwin and the other under a pen name. (Charlotte Ashe, after we moved from Weaverville to Charlotte Street in Asheville.)

There were haunting passages in the typescript. "From then on, my life will be borrowed from the night," Ann is musing about her coming blindness, just before the lights go out and the blue spot follows her disappearance out the window. How had the playwright come up with that lovely phrase?

And then this exchange, which made me ache for my mother all over again:

MRS. MCGINNIS: (Rising and crossing to JEAN and looking over her shoulder at the paper in the typewriter) What are you writing now?

JEAN: I'm trying to write another short story. It's not going so well, though. (With a sigh) I suppose it will end up like most of the others in some editor's wastebasket.

However, the wastebasket made my heart lift a little: maybe the playwright hadn't been sending out stories yet, or she *would have known* that editors always returned them—if you had enclosed your self-addressed stamped envelope, which I was sure Kathleen Krahenbuhl always would have done.

Poor *Windy Peaks* never got beyond those carefully labored over five pages the Knopf scout read in 1958 while the author stood beside her (on the left). I remember being thrilled by my opening: the mysterious young person on the make standing in the darkness, hitchhiking his way to the top. But I can see how I would have been arduously challenged by all those other characters, high and low, male and female, who still had to be invented.

Meanwhile, I had my courses to pass at Chapel Hill and I would need to apply for waitressing jobs for the coming summer. And I had my twice-weekly column, "Carolina Carousel," to write for the *Daily Tar Heel*. The smirking coed with her flying hair in the column's stamp-size photo was often recognized as she crossed the campus, and this was publication enough for a while. I would have to live through some humiliating failures before completing a first novel five years later.

Pursuit with Interruptions

UNHAPPY WIVES AT THE OCEAN'S EDGE

I.

Sometimes, late in the night, she would go into the kitchen to get a glass of water and stand by the dark window listening to the sounds of the crickets, and sometimes she would hear the distant blast of a steamship passing around the key and she would experience a feeling which she could not put into words . . . it was something like the feeling of missing a friend or a train by five minutes.

Gull Key (unpublished manuscript, 1962)

LONDON, 1964

Time was running out. When I looked at my face in London's mirrors, I was often startled that it wasn't an old face. In my imagination I already inhabited my future and in this future I was about fifty-five and nothing dramatic had happened. I was alone and working at some menial job in an overcast city to keep body and soul together.

And yet my life after Chapel Hill had been studded with drama: On assignment for a Miami newspaper, I had spent the night in jail with a woman who had murdered her husband and I had flown on a navy plane into the eye of a hurricane. I had been fired by the same newspaper, been married and divorced within the space of five months, sailed to Europe on a freighter, lived in Copenhagen and the Canary Islands, and, for the last two years, in London, where I worked at a glamorous menial government job that Cousin Bill (the mayor from Weaverville) had helped me get. But I felt no further along toward my goal than that downcast younger self trudging across campus after the Knopf turndown and realizing I was simply that year's model of a young person hungry for success.

But that wasn't totally true. Out of the ill-considered Miami marriage had come a 210-page novel, *Gull Key*, my take on *Madame Bovary* but owing more daily details to Somerset Maugham's *Mrs. Craddock*, whose heroine I felt closer to. Also Bertha Craddock read better books than did Emma Bovary. My novel had the added attraction of being set on the ocean—an island with a lighthouse, no less, which shared an ambience with Woolf's novel, which I had studied in that intensive course at Chapel Hill.

In my novel, a new wife was trapped on this Florida island, already realizing that being married was not the same as wanting to be married. The manuscript of *Gull Key* had been composed on the best typewriter in my life so far, on the third floor of the U.S. embassy in Grosvenor Square during the slow summer of 1962, while the permanent quarters of the United States Travel Service (USTS) were being readied for us at the corner of Sackville and Vigo, off Regent Street.

"There was so much time to write on that third floor!" I reminisced to my new colleague, Dorothea, between customers at our handsome new office. Dorothea and I presided behind a counter on the ground floor, which we called the "Fish Bowl" because the showroom was completely glassed in. We'd asked our boss to have panels built beneath the counter so people couldn't look up our skirts, and, gent that he was, he was crushed that he hadn't thought of it himself. "While we were over on Grosvenor Square," I told Dorothea, "most of our English customers preferred to write to us for information about travel in the States rather than come in person to the embassy, so I was able to finish my novel in three months. I don't think Mr. Miller minded, because I always looked so busy."

"Sharing their third floor with you for the summer must have driven the CIA crazy," laughed Dorothea. "All these tweedy mums and dads bumbling into their inner sanctum by mistake: 'Oh, I say, is this where I inquire about your ninety-nine-day bus ticket across America?'"

Dorothea had replaced my previous colleague, Pat, who had gone back to California to be married. Nixon, who had lost the presidential bid to Kennedy, had attended her wedding. Dorothea was a Radcliffe graduate who had campaigned for both Kennedy brothers when they were running for the Senate; now she was married to her English cousin, a psychiatrist, who made her bitterly unhappy. During slack periods in the Fish Bowl, we entertained each other with marital anecdotes. Dorothea's husband woke her up one night because she had failed to replace the cap on the toothpaste. I told, exaggerating a little, how I had finally got rid of my husband's overstaying houseguests by scheduling a fumigation by Orkin. Dorothea had read *Gull Key* and suggested I put in more humor. ("Like the stories you tell in the office.") One publisher and one agent had turned it down. The publisher, a Scotsman, invited me to his office, which was right around the corner from our office. He gave me a whisky in front of a crackling coal fire and explained he published only military books now, "but you have a way with *worruds* and I would like to send this over to my Anglo-American friend, Ursula, who is a literary agent. Her cousin was the very popular American ambassador here during the

War." The Anglo-American agent, a gracious, soft-spoken lady in middle age, gave me a cup of tea in front of a space heater and told me I had a lively narrative gift, though she feared *Gull Key* would not do well with English publishers. She offered to have a look at anything else I might write.

Then November 22, 1963, came. It was midday in Dallas and suppertime in London. I was at my Chelsea boardinghouse sitting down to the evening meal with the other young professionals (later memorialized in *Mr. Bedford*) when Andrew (Alexander in the novella) rushed in to announce he'd just heard on "the wireless" that the American president had been shot. "But he's still alive," Andrew reported, "and they will know how to save him." Then Dorothea was phoning me and asking me to get on the train to Dulwich and stay the night with her. The psychiatrist-husband met me at the station. By then Kennedy was dead and Johnson had been sworn in. We heard this on the radio. Dorothea's husband suggested the three of us play cards, to keep us steady, I suppose, but at last he went off to bed and Dorothea plunged into an eloquent tailspin of homesickness and grief.

Soon after, she bolted from Dulwich and returned to America.

"Don't stay over there too long," she scrawled on a postcard from her new job at an American Express in Boston.

"And don't, whatever you do, marry an Englishman or a psychiatrist!"

I signed up for an evening fiction writing course at the City Literary Institute in Holborn. The teacher, Miss Irene Slade, was a lovely lady who worked for the BBC in the daytime. She began by reading stories to us in her mellow broadcasting voice. The first was an early story by Chekhov, "Anyuta," and the next was "The Seraph and the Zambesi," the first story Muriel Spark ever wrote, which won a contest, convincing her she could be a writer. Miss Slade had high standards. She returned my first story with a note that said I wrote very engagingly, "but unfortunately I could not see the forest for the trees. There are simply too many asides that divert the flow." My story was about a quiet, middle-aged woman, sort of based on the Anglo-American literary agent, who works in a travel agency and sends others off to interesting destinations, but never goes anywhere herself. Miss Slade suggested that I write something from the point of view of a person *"quite* different from yourself," and I wrote a story about a shy English vicar who meets God during a solitary walk. He writes a book about his experience, becomes an international publishing success, and hits rock bottom while lecturing at a girls' college in the American South. Miss Slade loved it and asked me to read it aloud to the class. As soon as I began reading, I was overcome with snorts and guffaws and had to keep starting over to control my hilarity.

Afterward, a craggy, rumpled man who always carried his motor scooter helmet under his arm asked Miss Slade and me to join him at the pub next door. Within three months we were married. He was an English psychiatrist.

II.

He spoke in a low, persuasive voice, like a father or a teacher instructing children. His voice was years older than he was. There was something different about him. His craggy features, which could have been bucolic on another, were charged with a zealous, sensitive energy. His black hair had the carelessly combed look of a genius. His dark liquid eyes snapped and glistened from behind his glasses with the fire of one who has seen, and come back from, a vision.

For a long time, Dane had been on the lookout for, if not an actual vision, at least an event charged with meaning which would signal the turning point of her life.

The Perfectionists (1970, submitted in ms. as *The Beautiful French Family*)

IOWA CITY, 1968

Time had continued to run out, and though I had added a few more colorful chapters to my life history, I was no nearer my goal than that girl who couldn't stop guffawing while reading her story aloud to Miss Slade's fiction-writing class in Holborn. Well no, that wasn't completely true. The story about the English vicar, revised many times during the year and a half of my bleak and peculiar second marriage, got me into the Iowa Writers' Workshop. Kurt Vonnegut, my teacher, loved the forty-page story about the hellish Majorcan vacation of an English psychiatrist with his American wife and his three-year-old illegitimate son, who refuses to speak. It was called "The Beautiful French Family" because there was such a family, a reproach to my ill-matched family, staying at the hotel. "Nice," "First rate!" Vonnegut penciled in the margins. (Though he also penciled in things like "sand-bagging flashback!")

"Should I turn it into a novel?" I asked him in a conference. "No, it's fine the way it is," Vonnegut rasped from behind a cloud of cigarette smoke, his long, thin Hush Puppies propped on his desk. "Well, I decided to turn it into a novel," I informed him in our next conference. "Hey, that's great!" he said. As a teacher, Kurt Vonnegut was easy, magnanimous. He didn't try to make his students into little Kurt Vonneguts. He respected material unlike his own and was startlingly humble about what he did. ("I write with a big black crayon," he would write to me later, "while you're more of an impressionist. I don't think you have it in you to be crude.") In his workshop sessions, things always seemed a little looser, a little kinder, a little funnier. In May 1967 he would leave Iowa on a Guggenheim grant to do research in Dresden for *Slaughterhouse-Five*, his novel in progress, but all that spring I chugged along in creative bliss. A writer I admired had given me the go-ahead. I wrote into the late night and early morning in my Iowa City rooms across the street from the jail, wrote about another wife on an island for whom marriage was not at all like she had imagined. I finished the novel in June, and a New York agent expressed an interest in representing it if I would rewrite it, which I spent the summer doing. But the agent was disappointed in the new draft and regretfully declined to take me on. She said it was too tendentious and not as appealing as the first draft. After looking up *tendentious* in the dictionary I thought I could smooth out any heavy-handed passages, but how did you go about putting back the appeal in something?

When you were down, it seemed, the insults piled up. Or maybe you were just more vulnerable to them. When I went to renew my driver's license, the woman on duty frowned at it, then summoned an Iowa state trooper, who led me out in the hall for a talk.

"This birth date has been tampered with," he said.

"I know. I'm sorry."

"Why did you do it?"

"Because. I didn't want to be thirty."

Thank God for the gift of tears and for kind state troopers old enough to be your father.

I gave the new (rejected) draft to my next workshop teacher, who promised to read it as soon as duck hunting season was over. In early December, he told me he had finally read it on a long airplane flight and hadn't warmed to it much.

"Do you think I'll ever make it as a writer?" I was desperate enough to plead.

"Gee, Gail, how old are you?"

"Thirty," I humbly croaked.

"Well, I don't know," he said, looking sad for me. "I was twenty-four when I published my first novel."

After the conference with the duck hunter, I entered the Ph.D. program. If I could not be a published writer, maybe I could earn my living teaching literature until I was sixty-five and then I would decide whether I wanted to go on living. To prove myself to the English Department, I agreed to teach an early morning course, Greek Drama for

Freshmen Engineers, which was the maverick idea of a tenured professor whom the other professors looked down on because he had written his dissertation on Baron Corvo. Having made a success of this experiment, I was awarded a scholarship and assigned to teach the conventional core lit courses. But those Greek plays, which I had read for the first time the night before bewitching the young engineers while the blood was still fresh in my mind, remained my consummate teaching triumph.

I abandoned the duck hunter for a new workshop teacher, Robert Coover, who announced on the first day of class that he intended to change the shape of American fiction. Students called him the Little Magician. The William Faulkner Foundation had just given Best First Novel award to his *Origin of the Brunists*, and his classes were stimulating and full of camaraderie. He passed out blue books. "Okay, here's our setup for today: a fourth-century monk has discovered a new tale by Scheherazade in a codex. Write it however you like, from the monk's point of view, or you can write Scheherazade's tale . . . or parts of it." I was very pleased with my exercise. Having fallen in love with Anglo-Saxon poetry and all things medieval in my graduate courses, I wrote from the point of view of a young monk on the island of Lindisfarne. His fingers are cold as he draws pictures in the margins of the manuscript. He doesn't know anything about Arabs or Scheherazade, but he likes his drawings and decides to draw the brave little bird singing in the winter cold outside the walls of the scriptorium.

At the end of class the Little Magician collected the blue books, and the following week he passed out mimeographs of a compilation of the abridged contents, arranged by himself. My young monk had made the cut, but he was now part of a metafictional collage. The aim of the modern writer, Coover told us, was to subvert the traditional text and to challenge linearity. "If you as Author are free to take a story anywhere, at any time, and in as many directions as you want, isn't that your obligation?"

God, no, I thought. But I asked him to read my novel about the unhappy Majorcan vacation: as my teacher it was his obligation. He read it promptly and told me it was publishable and urged me not to seek publication. "It will attract the wrong readers and you'll be relegated to the domestic-social novelist slot."

The conference with Coover somehow energized me, and I wrote two stories in a week. The first, "St. George," was a contemporary story about a lonely graduate student, Gwen, who cracks an egg and finds a tiny dragon and tries to raise it in her apartment. The second, "The Sorrowful Mother," was written as a tale about a nameless wife and mother who has sequential nightmares about being in a small boat with her husband and little boy and wishing them all dead. As the dreams intensify, she withdraws from her husband and child into a room of her own. When a subsequent dream reveals that they will die in the boat, she waits until they are out of the house and goes on a creative binge. Then she takes a lethal draft and smashes them all to pieces in her final dream. The husband and child return home to a dead mother and a houseful of loving drawings and poems and food.

"You thought I'd like the dragon story best, didn't you?" said Coover, "but you surpassed yourself in 'The Sorrowful Mother.' You have taken this subject as far as it can go. It has a domestic setting, but it is not a domestic story."

Later I will tell you the fate of this story, which was to become the much-anthologized "A Sorrowful Woman."

As for "St. George," it has had a long life as a Selected Short at Symphony Space, read by Jane Curtin (one of the founders of *Saturday Night Live*). It is available on a CD (*Pets!*) and was recently reintroduced by Stephen Colbert. For years I had shied away from recordings of my work because of the "southern accents" the producers made the actors imitate. But last year I finally listened to Curtin's "St. George" (no southern accent) and laughed myself silly. It was astonishing how much an actor with great timing could bring to a written tale.

It was now the fall of 1968, and I wrote for long hours, sometimes late into the night, in my basement office at EPB, as we called the English-Philosophy Building. I had moved fifteen blocks north of campus to a nicer upstairs apartment in a beautiful old Victorian house, but it was too far to walk for meals, so I ate in the student cafeteria. I began a third draft of the Majorcan vacation novel, trying to make it less domestic and social. I got them through customs, then threw out the lifeless pages and treated myself to a respite of clean despair. I would do my job each day, teach my core classes, go to my graduate classes, fulfill my assignments, write my stories for the Little Magician, write because I couldn't help writing, but live without publishing hopes.

In the morning I walked the fifteen blocks to EPB without publishing hopes and at night I walked back to the rooms that were laid out like those of Gwen the lonely graduate student who had fed St. George the dragon Woolworth pearls until he grew too big for the apartment. As the author of that story I had been able to resolve how Gwen could free a dragon the size of a small bear into a more suitable environment and get on with her life, but I couldn't see a way out of my own dilemma. Writing had lived inside me since I was a little girl, and the need to write had continued to grow like a beast, but how to give it the room it needed and not become a bitter human being?

Unpublished Prosperities

OBSCURITY AND BREAKTHROUGH

When we compare the present life of man with that time of which we have no knowledge, it seems to me like the swift flight of a lone sparrow through the banqueting-hall where you sit in the winter months to dine with your thanes and counsellors. Inside there is a comforting fire to warm the room; outside, the wintry storms of snow and rain are raging. This sparrow flies swiftly in through one door of the hall, and out through another. While he is inside, he is safe from the winter storms; but after a few moments of comfort, he vanishes from sight into the darkness whence he came.

Bede, *A History of the English Church and People*

(A.D. 731), translated by Leo Sherley-Price (1955)

"So? What do I risk? Obscurity?"

This riposte, which a fiction workshop student flung back at her peers after their critique of her story in the spring of 1967, just after I arrived in Iowa City, reverberated through the fourth-floor halls of EPB and was quoted with awe and respect by her colleagues.

I was not in that workshop, but my friend Lorraine O'Grady had been in it, and Lorraine was a reliable narrator.

"That's exactly what she said," Lorraine told me. "After they finished tearing her story apart because it was too 'obscure' and nobody would publish it, she stood up and said in that husky deadpan voice of hers, 'So? What do I risk? Obscurity?' Just like that. You could have heard a pin drop."

Lorraine, whom I had met in 1961 after a Marian Anderson concert in Copenhagen and stayed in touch with ever since, had urged me to come to Iowa and "get serious" about my writing; she had personally delivered my English vicar story to the faculty member in charge of admissions. ("Your friend has some kinks," Eugene Garber, the metaphysical tale writer, told Lorraine, "but we can work them out of her.") Lorraine had entered the workshop two years before me to become a novelist but ended up translating her teacher José Donoso's novel *Este Domingo* (*This Sunday*) into English instead. She went on to make her living as a translator and a teacher until she burst like a guerrilla rocket on the New York conceptual art scene in 1980 as Mlle Bourgeoise Noire, a black debutante in a white ball gown who crashes art openings in defiance of the current convention, which at that time kept the black and white art worlds segregated. Since then Lorraine O'Grady has become a performance pioneer in her field. The morning after I met her at the American ambassador's house in Copenhagen, I started a novel about her. It was titled *Roxanne O'Day*. Roxanne was to be the star, and Carrie (my role) would function as the dazzled Nick Carraway narrator. They have just been introduced by the cultural attaché at the American ambassador's house. Roxanne is all in white, Carrie all in black. ("Here you are, two American girls traveling solo," said the attaché. "What did you think of the concert?" Anticipating this question, Carrie delivered the answer she had prepared during the concert: "What a majestic voice. I felt honored to be in that hall." Roxanne said: "Well, of course she's incomparable. However, I don't think she should have sung quite so much German in this country, if you know what I mean.")

When Lorraine and I reconnected by e-mail in 2012 after I saw photographs of her new show in the *New York Times*, I decided to devote a chapter to her in *Publishing*. I was going to call the chapter "Embodying Your Art," which is what Lorraine does. Mlle Bourgeoise Noire wore a floor-length dress made of hundreds of white gloves sewn together by herself. In her May 2012 show there is a twenty-minute black-and-white video entitled *Landscape*

(Western Hemisphere), which at first seems to show a field of blowing weeds; but it is a close-up of Lorraine O'Grady's African American hair being blown between two fans. In both my attempts to write about her, the abandoned 1961 Copenhagen novel and the abandoned chapter for this book, my narrative powers were outdone by Lorraine's reality.

I knew by sight that workshop student with the husky deadpan voice, a raven-haired tomboy loner, similar in looks to MSNBC's Rachel Maddow today, though swarthier and always unsmiling. I have tried to recall her name. I'm sure I would have written it in my journal, along with the famous obscurity quote, but that particular journal was thrown into the Iowa River by a jealous boyfriend determined to destroy everything that came before him.

I don't know whether that workshop student went on to publish her "obscure" story in a literary quarterly, or whether she ever published at all. But she has remained my beau ideal for a last-ditch pigheadedness essential to a writer's day-to-day endurance. When my inner naysayers start chipping away at me for risking something—or even thinking of risking something—I fling back the tomboy loner's retort, and it restores perspective.

So? What do I risk? Obscurity? became my mantra during that Iowa autumn of 1968, as I marched the fifteen blocks to and from my apartment on North Dubuque Street.

By 1968, most of my close circle had moved on. Lorraine went to Chicago, where she was translating a nineteenth-century German prostitute's memoirs into English and Hugh Hefner's daily menus into French for his chef.

John Irving had moved back east with his wife and first child, Colin, to take a teaching job. I had met John when Jane Barnes and John Casey and David Plimpton took me with them to Irving's twenty-fifth birthday party. In his small apartment, John showed us the writing room he had made for himself in a coat closet. For his birthday guests he played a tape of the "film score" for his first novel, *Setting Free the Bears*. He hadn't finished the novel yet, no publisher or movie person had laid eyes on it, but John had chosen the music he wanted, from Carl Orff's *Carmina Burana*. ("I often did that," John told me many years later. "I picked the music for my film before I finished the book. Call it my mayhem confidence.")

David Plimpton, having published a first story before any of us, about a young man on the verge of his future, in *Penthouse*, had gone back east for graduate study in psychology. John Casey had married Jane Barnes and they were finishing their M.F.A. degrees at the workshop. Casey had just sold his first story to the *New Yorker* about his time in the army. Jane, who was in Coover's class with me, was expecting a baby in December.

The other recitation that sustained me on my fifteen-block walks between EPB and the house on North Dubuque Street was lines from the Anglo-Saxon poem "The Wanderer." ("Though the correct translation of *anhaga* is not 'wanderer' but 'he who is solitarily situated,'" Professor McGalliard had explained to us.)

> *Hwaer cwom mearg? Hwaer cwom mago?*
> *Hwaer cwom maþþumgyfa?*
> *Hwaer cwom symbla gesetu?*
> *Hwaer sindon seledreamas?*

> Where is the horse gone? Where the rider?
> Where the giver of treasure?
> Where are the seats at the feast?
> Where are the revels in the hall?

And then came the hopeless lines that I loved best:

> Alas for the bright cup!
> Alas for the mailed warrior!
> Alas for the splendour of the prince!
> How that time has passed away,

all under the cover of night,

as if it had never been!

It was all going to pass away for everybody! Whether I was
the warrior with the gold cup or Bede's little sparrow darting
through the banqueting hall, we were all going to vanish,
every last one of us, published or unpublished, back into the
night from whence we came. This never failed to cheer me
up. Unlike the aloof stars high above the Blue Ridge
Mountains or the scrubbed-out stars over pink-lit London or
smoggy New York, the low-hanging stars over Iowa winked
and signaled with pre-Copernican intimacy. The Anglo-
Saxon Wanderer (or "he who is solitarily situated,") would
have felt right at home under this sky.

I was "she who is solitarily situated," on my night walks,
marching to the beat of a doomed language.

In the early morning of October 2, 1968, I dreamed there
was a house where my future was. It was horribly dirty and
sooty. I went down a hall and turned right into a living
room—substandard furniture, filthy, no books—a young
blond boy loitering. "Do you know if there are any books
here?" I asked. He said, "No, but downstairs." He showed
me how to descend a ladder to the floor below, and there was

Anglo-Saxon banqueting hall

"Whether I was the warrior with the gold cup or Bede's little sparrow
darting through the banqueting hall, we were all going to vanish."

a library of boring old books. I went into other rooms. Each room got cleaner till at last I found a neat study, and on its shelves I found one thin book that I had written. Its title was *Unpublished Prosperities.*

It was an affecting dream, but what did it mean? Was I literally headed for "unpublished prosperity" for the rest of my life, or was the dream telling me something in its own code?

Two fiction workshop students had a young agent in New York, John Hawkins, who worked for the old, esteemed firm of Paul R. Reynolds, which had represented Henry James, George Bernard Shaw, H. G. Wells, and Willa Cather. Hawkins had read both their manuscripts in progress and told them he would send out their work when they had completed "fifty good pages." The first student, from the Philippines, Willie Nolledo, had gone on to finish his novel and Hawkins had sold it. The second, who tended to fall in love with newly discovered words, like *tessellations*, was still perfecting his first fifty pages.

The prospect seemed less onerous when the goal was "fifty good pages." With this magic number in sight, I started over, trying to forget the disappointments and wrong turnings of my publishing attempts and focus on my ill-matched couple, whose disappointments and wrong turnings were not going to be as easy to conceal under the bright scrutiny of the island's sun. The more I wrote about the little boy who will not speak, the more I realized that his maddening silence was a reflection on the unspoken falseness of their whole situation. They were never going to be the family they wanted others to think they were. They were never going to be like the beautiful French family staying in their hotel. In fact, I was still calling the novel *The Beautiful French Family*.

When I had four chapters (which came to forty-eight pages), I mailed them in a manila envelope (with stamped return envelope enclosed) to John Hawkins, who wrote back that he was fascinated by the pages and would like to represent me. "I know I shouldn't ask," he said, "but I am curious to know how old you are, and whether you are English or American."

He got to work immediately. The publisher William Morrow offered $250 for an option on the forty-eight pages, but Hawkins wrote that he thought we could do better. (How nice it was to be a "we"!) He said the Morrow offer was an encouraging nod, but not as binding as a contract. He would like to try other publishers.

I had a vivid dream of going to a bookstore with the Little Magician. Coover was dressed in tights like a court jester and was scolding me for neglecting to update the class bulletin board, which he took great pride in because it was an extension of his personality. I told him that if we were going to do the board justice we would need to buy some beautiful colored letters in porcelain for it, and led him into an extension of the store that sold knickknacks. There he became smitten with a little glass elephant with a rider, which I encouraged him to buy. But it cost more than he had and I felt bad.

When I woke up I knew there was going to be bad news in my EPB mailbox, and there was. Hawkins had enclosed a rejection letter from an editor at Random House. ("She's a born storyteller, but the subject and location of this book are just too remote and I fear we couldn't sell enough copies.") John had written "Onward and Upward!" above his signature.

Back down into hopelessness once more, which at least felt more familiar, I walked to the university in winter cold, read *The Owl and the Nightingale* in Middle English, taught my core class *King Lear* and played for them on a record the part near the end when Cordelia awakens Lear (Paul Scofield) and he thinks she is a spirit:

> You do me wrong to take me out o' th' grave;
> Thou art a soul in bliss; but I am bound
> Upon a wheel of fire, that mine own tears
> Do scald like molten lead.

I wrote the next chapter of my remote novel that wouldn't sell enough copies, and trudged home under the starlit canopy of obscurity.

"You've still got us," my mother said on the phone. "Come for Christmas."

"But, I was just there last summer."

"Well, come again."

That summer, walking through the neighborhood where we had lived when Kathleen Godwin was also Charlotte Ashe when she had more than one story in an issue, we had returned to our favorite topic, writing and getting published, a topic that never failed to charge my mother's voice with a youthful wistfulness. She hadn't stopped writing, even after the love pulps had seen their day. She wrote novels, under the name Mary Godwin, one after the other, after she remarried—a GI taking one of her English classes at Asheville-Biltmore College—and had three more children. My favorite of her novels was (and remains) *The Otherwise Virgins*, about three quite different coeds on the Chapel Hill campus after World War II: the promiscuous Lisa; the withdrawn Jane, who loves women; and Debby, an older student, a former call girl in New York. In some ways it was ahead of its time. Nobody wanted to think about Jane's problem, and they found the ex–call girl adopted by the southern senator beyond belief. Her agent, Ann Elmo, kept faith with Mary Godwin through the years. My mother and I could recite by heart the entire letter forwarded to her by Elmo in December 1949:

Miss Ann Elmo

AFG Literary Agency

545 Fifth Avenue

New York 17, New York

My dear Ann:

I do not know Mary Godwin but, in spots, she writes like the angels. In others, she hits notes of monstrous tedium calculated to repel the most ardent reader.

I'm not going to buy "And Not to Yield." I might have if the classroom scenes were not so long; and if, perhaps Allen and Ravenelle could refrain from blaspheming the romantic couch with recitations from Shakespeare's Sonnets and the Rubaiyat. The best thing she could do is to pare the fat from this. It comes to 135,000 words and would read beautifully at 90,000.

Still, Miss Godwin is one hell of a writer. If she lives nearby, I'd be happy to take her to lunch and talk about a book for us.

A Merry Christmas to you . . .
Jim Bishop
Editor
Fawcett Gold Medal Books

We had a little duet for our refrain:

"Writes like the angels!" (soprano)

"With notes of monstrous tedium!"(alto)

"Merry Christmas to you!" (soprano)

"If you pare the fat!" (alto)

On our final walk around the old streets last summer, we had been discussing Colin Wilson's funny autobiographical novel, *Adrift in Soho*, about young aspiring writers, artists, and anarchists hanging out in London after World War II. I had read it first, on the bus trip to Asheville, and passed it on to her.

"I enjoyed it so much," she said. "And you know what I loved best? Some of them are so close to fulfilling their dreams of being artists or published writers and they don't know how close. But *we* do!"

Tuesday, December 10, 1968, Iowa City was iced in. The day before, Jane Barnes Casey had given birth to a little girl, Maud. I had intended to walk to campus and write in my office, but then looked out my window, saw cars and people slipping and sliding all over the place, and decided to stay home and grade papers and wash my hair in the bathtub where St. George the dragon had slept and frolicked until he grew too big.

Around six in the evening, Kim Merker, the hand printer who had his press in the basement of EPB and an office next to mine, phoned. "There are all these notes stuck to your door to call your agent."

"I guess it's too late to call him now," I said. "If it's anything urgent, he'll have my home number."

As soon as I hung up, John Hawkins phoned. Yes, he was still at his office. An oral storyteller himself, he insisted on narrating the day's news chronologically. David Segal, an editor at Harper & Row, had read the forty-eight pages and outline of *The Beautiful French Family* and wanted to meet with John and discuss it. Over lunch at the Brussels, he'd offered fifteen hundred dollars for an option on the book. Over dessert (crème brûlée), John had said, "Gail would be so much happier with fifteen hundred dollars and a contract," and David had agreed.

"Will a delivery date of May 1969 give you enough time?" John asked.

I made long-distance calls to Ian Marshall, the psychiatrist in London, Lorraine O'Grady in Chicago, and John Bowers in New York, who was working on his

A scholar's reading room inside Wilson Library
Where Gail's papers are archived today.

autobiographical novel, *The Colony* (1971) about a young man learning to write at the Handy Writers' Colony in Illinois.

"It's what you wanted," said Ian, "and I'm glad. But you still owe me your airfare back to America."

"Good God," said Lorraine. "Look, you've got to give me a moment to take this in."

John Bowers was overjoyed. "See? See? Didn't I always tell you?"

I had saved the most important phone call for last.

"Now when you come for Christmas we will really have something to celebrate," my mother said. "I know what this means, believe me. And you know I know what it means."

Publishing Partners

Two basic questions the editor should be addressing to the author are: Are you saying what you want to say? and, Are you saying it as clearly and consistently as possible? If these sound narrow at first glance, think further. They cover everything from awkward syntax and repetition to the destruction of a novel's impact through a protagonist's behavior so unexplained and unmotivated as to be unintentionally baffling. All this is of course subject to free and extended discussion and the author is the ultimate arbiter, as all responsible editors would agree. They would also concur that knowing when to leave things alone is as high an editorial skill as knowing when to suggest revision.

Does all this always work out in a glow of amity and constructive engagement? Certainly not, no more frequently than do love affairs. Overbearing, insensitive editors and mulish, unlistening authors, whether singly or in pairs, have caused many a shift of contract

*and failed book. Both species eventually tend to meet
comeuppance and run out of partners.*

Alan D. Williams, "What Is an Editor?" in *Editors on
Editing*, 3d ed., edited by Gerald Gross, Grove Press

Copying out those words for the preceding epigraph, I appreciated Alan Williams anew, with the added refinement that time can bring. These paragraphs are so like him, so like his editing notes and his style of editing a manuscript. Everything is there, only he's not going to hit you over the head with it. Read his assessment, read it again, "think further," and you begin to extract its full wisdom and bite. It's fitting that he can still bestow his editing gifts on me from the grave: in this instance giving me the image of a dance partnership for the relationship between an author and her editors.

On a publishing dance card, my partners would appear in this order:

1. David Segal
2. Robert Gottlieb
3. Alan Williams
4. Harvey Ginsberg
5. Linda Grey
6. Jennifer Hershey
7. Nancy Miller

8. Jennifer Hershey

9. Nancy Miller

My first partner, the one who went to lunch at the Brussels with John Hawkins, died before our dance ever got in full swing. In May 1970 David saw *The Perfectionists* through publication at Harper & Row. When he contracted for that novel, he had offered to guide me through the rest of the manuscript, or let me find my own way, and I chose to go it alone. When he received the finished manuscript he mailed me his notes, including a major suggestion that I resisted. But at the last moment, he and John Hawkins talked me out of murdering a character on the last page. (It was the right decision.) David then moved to Knopf as a senior fiction editor and we signed a contract for a second novel, *The Angel Keeper*, about a young American woman putting off her American marriage and getting caught up in the sinister goings-on in the household of her London employer, an Anglican priest, and his mad sister and a manipulative housekeeper. ("David has flipped over *The Angel Keeper*," reported Hawkins.) However David had some suggestions and qualms about the setup of this novel: how was I going to sustain the American side, which, by page 90, wasn't as interesting as the English side? We had made a date to discuss this over a long lunch on December 28, when, armed with my brand-new

Ph.D., I would be in New York applying for teaching jobs at the Modern Language Association convention.

The morning of the twenty-eighth, a Monday, began on a note of anxiety. I lurked in my hotel room at the Americana and listened to the constant phone-ringing and opening and shutting of doors across the hall, where a university had taken an interviewing suite. To calm myself I started transcribing in my journal what I was overhearing from the hall.

Knock knock

(no answer)

Knock knock

(Door opens) Yes? (rather angrily)

Hello, I'm . . . mumble.

Oh, yes. Happy to meet you. Would you mind waiting outside for just a few more minutes? We're still . . . mumble, mumble.

Oh, sorry, I . . .

(Door slams. Some seconds go by. We hear the unclicking of the candidate's briefcase. Checking his vita sheet to make sure he still exists?)

Whenever I had something important to prepare for, I paced myself. Bathe and meditate on event ahead; prepare answers if necessary. Write in journal. Slowly dress. Apply makeup. I was still in pajamas and robe, having set my room service tray outside the door. That's when I saw the "University of Indiana" sign posted on the door opposite. I myself had a job interview with that institution in midafternoon. Was it a good sign or a bad sign that their suite was right across the hall? At least I now knew better than to knock on the door too early, like that last unfortunate candidate. Also I would be coming directly from lunch with my editor; how many job applicants could breeze in fresh from a lunch with their editor?

The phone rang and it was an old UNC classmate, Frank Crowther. He lived in Greenwich Village, was on the masthead of the *Paris Review*, and was working on a long novel, *What if Laughter Were Tears?*, which he had begun back in Chapel Hill after getting out of the Marines.

"So you're here. Come downtown and I'll treat you to lunch at the Red Lion."

"I'm having lunch with my editor at Knopf today."

"Who is your editor?"

"David Segal."

"But—he just died."

"That's not very funny, Frank."

"You haven't seen this morning's *Times*?"

"No. What—"

A rustle of newspaper on his end; in a subdued voice he began to read:

David I. Segal, a senior editor of Alfred A. Knopf, Inc., publishers, who was known for his encouragement of talented new authors, died yesterday, apparently of a heart attack, at his home, 280 Riverside Drive. He was 42 years old.

So instead of lunch with my editor, I was taken by my agent to meet the editor in chief and publisher at Knopf, who would assign me a new editor. (John Hawkins had been trying to get through to me while I was still listening to Frank reading David's obituary.)

"What kind of editor would you like to work with?" was Robert Gottlieb's first question to me in his office, and I replied rather pompously, "Well, it will have to be someone who appreciates great literature," then burst into sobs.

I still cringe when I recall this unfortunate opening to our nine-year partnership, but then I remind myself:

1. The first person who took a chance on publishing me had just died in his sleep. David had come out to Iowa with Hawkins to meet me, and I had been charmed by this fat little man, so at home with

himself, who loved books and told me I had a rare way of conveying "a sense of wrong."

2. Only one week before, I had passed my Ph.D. comprehensives and was still stuffed to the gills with Great Literature.

3. I had no teaching job for next year and no savings in the bank and the future looked bleak, especially with my champion dead.

"Yes, Gail, you were crying the first time I met you," Bob Gottlieb was to remind me more than once during our partnership, which had its affable periods and rocky moments.

"Some marriages are not made in heaven," Gottlieb would later reflect about our time together in his 1994 *Paris Review* interview with Larissa MacFarquhar ("The Art of Editing"), but on that late 1970 December day , he waited out my sobs and then said kindly, in response to my Great Literature stipulation, "Well, Gail, I'm afraid that's going to be me."

Bob Gottlieb guided and endured me through four books, two of which—*The Odd Woman* (1974) and *Violet Clay* (1978)—were finalists for the National Book Award. He wrote one of my recommendations for a Guggenheim fellowship, which I got, and he wrote a letter of protest to Larry McMurtry when McMurtry trashed *The Odd Woman* in a review. When I turned in an early version of something still called *The Angel Keeper* but with a vastly changed story from the one David had "flipped over" (it would later become *Glass People*), Bob wrote me a long letter, which ended, "Please Gail, I don't want you to ruin your chances," and so I dispensed with my wonderfully researched science-fiction ending of Cameron Bolt taking back his wife, Francesca, without realizing that the returned version was a high-quality robot.

Having read Great Literature, Bob could always catch me out when I had someone say "as you so beautifully do," or allowed a character to sunbathe naked next to a sleeping snake.

After I had turned in *The Odd Woman*, he urged me to add one more thing: "The reader needs to know whether Jane wants to have children. I think you must make this clear. Being a mother completely changes a woman's life."

Jane Clifford, a thirty-two-year-old English professor having an affair with a married man, wants tenure and she wants love, but I hadn't given a single thought to whether she wanted to be a mother. At the time I was thirty-six and hadn't quite made up my mind on that subject, but most days I did not see myself as a potential mother. However, Jane was not a paper doll of me—she wasn't a fiction writer, for instance—and I found a way to work out her feelings on the subject by having her, toward the end of the novel, when she has just decided to leave her married lover, make a list of the fates of the five single women featured in George Gissing's 1893 novel, *The Odd Women*, which she has been reading. It was fitting for the scholarly Jane to make a list of this kind and then apply it to her life.

> Compromise—rebellion against compromise—death
> Escape through drink—rehabilitation to "useful member of society"
> Finding fulfillment through "others"
> Sublimation of personal furies into "a cause"
> Starting all over again in a child

The whole passage, like a little personal essay, ran eight pages in a late chapter of *The Odd Woman*. (I still think the novel would have been fine without it, but maybe it made a difference to some readers.) Jane ends up drawing a line through every word on the list, except "a child," concluding with this open-ended fillip:

> And who knew: though she might never conceive him, she might dream him, sitting in front of her old-maid fire, as Charles Lamb had sat in front of his, telling wonderful stories to her unborn child.

I was to follow up on this idea of "Dream Children" in a later story, my first ghost story, which was also the title of the volume of stories I published with Knopf two years later, in 1976.

While I was checking some dates and facts for this chapter, I looked up Gottlieb and came across his *Paris Review* interview about the art of editing, which I had somehow missed.

"Some marriages are not made in heaven," the part about our time together began.

> Now, Gail was extremely sensitive, and she viewed herself as a highly successful commercial writer, whereas I viewed her as a rather literary writer with a limited readership. She couldn't live that way, and eventually, although we worked together very cordially on several books, she moved to Viking. She had shown them a book she was working on, and they saw it the way she saw it— as a major commercial novel—and they paid her a lot of money, and indeed it became a big best-seller and made her famous and successful. I didn't read her that way, and I still feel that her earlier work, which was less commercial, is more interesting. But she wanted to develop in a

different direction, and I'm sure she doesn't feel that she compromised in any way to do that. In other words, I was the wrong editor-publisher for her and she was wise to leave me.

But that's not how it happened, I thought. How could anyone have gotten me so wrong? I viewed myself as a literary writer who wanted to reach a larger audience and make enough money to take time off from teaching. The events leading up to my leaving Knopf played out with more intricacy and complexity than indicated by Gottlieb's recollections.

He was the first and only publisher to whom John Hawkins and I gave the first six chapters (250 pages, a third of what would be the finished novel) of *A Mother and Two Daughters*. Bob read it fast; he had never kept me waiting. "Listen, I like this," he said, "and it's fun to read." He said he loved novels about families and that being an only child had made him a sucker for anything about siblings. He thought I had set up the three women just right: "I don't mind stopping the sisters to read about Nell [the mother] and you shouldn't either." He said he'd given me up for lost the past eighteen months and for us to keep in close touch as I got nearer to the end, because "I know an author doesn't like to finish a book and have their editor gone." Then he called Hawkins and offered an advance of twenty-five thousand dollars, slightly more than he had paid for *Violet Clay*.

I anguished for several days. I knew that an advance is usually divided into four parts: a fourth on signing the contract, a fourth on manuscript delivery, a fourth on hardcover publication, a fourth on paperback publication. Sometimes there is a fifth part: final payment six months after paperback publication. I had hoped to bring in enough cash to let me go two years without teaching. I had been teaching at Vassar, and, at present, was teaching at Columbia. Six thousand a year minus agent's commission wouldn't pay for a year. Also, if I accepted Gottlieb's offer, no other publishers would ever see the book. On the other hand, I liked being a Knopf author, something I had aspired to ever since the Knopf scout turned down my five pages in Chapel Hill in 1958; and I liked it when people asked, "Who is your editor?" and exclaimed, "Oh, he's the best in the business," when I told them. Nevertheless I told John Hawkins to decline the offer, and we started putting together a list of publishers I wanted to try.

"I've had a rather curious talk with Gottlieb," John reported the day after. He had called Bob and told him we were declining because I needed a larger advance to live for two years without teaching. Bob had told Hawkins he just couldn't go any higher and maybe we should look somewhere else. "Then," John said, "I asked Bob, 'If we don't get what we want, can we come back?' And Bob said, 'Gail is always welcome to come back. But wait . . . what do I get out of this? *You're* leaving *me*. Let's say that I get a chance to match the highest bidder. If Gail gets a hundred thousand dollars, God bless her she should take it and go, but say someone offers thirty-five thousand, I'd like to see if I can talk to one of the paperback houses and then match the offer.'"

John sent manuscripts to Atlantic Monthly Press; Doubleday; Farrar, Straus & Giroux; Morrow; Putnam; Simon & Schuster; and Viking.

Aaron Asher at Farrar, Straus was the first to call. "We don't usually go after Knopf authors," he said, but when John told him Gottlieb had agreed to let me test the market and wanted to be in on the bidding, Asher said, "In that case, I'd love to have this book on our list. I don't know if I can afford it but I'd like to have it."

Seven houses besides Knopf wanted to publish *A Mother and Two Daughters*. Viking, Doubleday, and Simon & Schuster stayed in the bidding until the end, and Viking won with a fifty-five-thousand-dollar offer. (Bob Wyatt at Avon had backed the deal with an offer for the paperback, which, in turn, would lead to another auction.)

When recalling today that seven major New York houses were bidding for my book while Robert Starer, the composer with whom I shared my life, and I were crossing on the ferry to Ocracoke, I feel there are still three of me in one skin and none of us can quite believe it. There is the author on the ferry, on her way to revisit the island where *A Mother and Two Daughters* will reach its denouement, which she hasn't written yet; there is the unpublished student chanting Anglo-Saxon poetry on her solitary walk home under the Iowa stars; and there is the present me, who sits here at the keyboard in Woodstock, in the house that was built on the bounty that had its beginnings on that day.

Robert and I landed on Ocracoke, and I called Hawkins from a pay phone. The auction was over. But first John had had to call Gottlieb, as promised, and he had just gotten off the phone with him. "Gail must call me herself and tell me she wants to be published by me," Gottlieb had told John. "Then I might top Viking's offer. Or I might not. I haven't decided yet."

"So, it's up to you," said John. "Do you need time to think it over?"

"No, I have already decided," I said.

Robert and I had discussed it at length during our drive from Woodstock to North Carolina's Outer Banks.

"I want to start over," I told John, "with an editor who is over the moon to have won me."

And that is my side of the story of how Bob and I came to the end of our dance.

Alan Williams at Viking was the first editor with whom I finally got to have lunch. He had been at Viking for two decades, as both managing editor and editorial director.

I didn't meet him until after he had read the completed manuscript of *A Mother and Two Daughters*. In those bygone days, publishing wasn't shut down between Christmas and New Year's, and on December 31, the last day of 1980, I took the seven thirty A.M. bus from Woodstock to New York so I could arrive at Viking a little past ten: a whole new beginning. The lobby of 625 Madison was blazing with pots of red and white poinsettias. After a final going-over with my hairbrush, I took the elevator to the sixteenth floor. Alan Williams, stocky, with thick white hair, blue eyes, and a young face for his age—fresh in its quality of expectancy to be enlightened or entertained— took me to meet his colleagues: publisher Irv Goodman, editor Amanda Vaill, marketing director Connie Sayre, publicity director Victoria Meyer, and subsidiary rights editor Jean Griffin. All of them had read *A Mother and Two Daughters*, and each talked of their department's plans for it. It was a publishing first for me: meeting so many people all at once who were excited about working with me on my book.

We went to Alan's office, overflowing with books and manuscripts that toppled onto several of the faded green slipcovered chairs. Over coffee Alan said that he had read my manuscript during the weekend before Christmas and it had been like living two lives, "only the life of your book seemed more real." At Princeton Christmas parties, he kept looking for people like Lucy, the ex-congressman's wife who precedes her husband into parties smiling and blinking like the little flasher cars that precede oversize vehicles on the highway.

We then adjourned to a conference room where we sat next to each other at a big table and went through the manuscript. He had written notes on a legal pad and, for an hour and a half, he suggested large and small clarifications, corrected grammar and syntax, and also pointed out things he had especially loved: the opening party, the theological argument between Cate and her mother's clergyman friend, the names of certain characters, like the wild divorcée, Taggart McCord. His attention to detail was extraordinary. Wouldn't rich Roger Jernigan have bought his handicapped son a state-of-the-art telescope to watch the passing traffic on the Mississippi River from the bluff outside their castle? Would a pile of *National*

Geographics burn more slowly than old newspapers in a house fire?

After that, we walked to a Japanese restaurant where it was private and dark and talked about writers we admired and those we thought were overrated. He told me about his three daughters, one of whom had just published her first story in *Redbook*, and I told him about my mother and her writing and about Robert.

I sometimes wonder how things would have gone if I could have had more time working with Alan. But the publishing industry was on the threshold of drastic upheavals, and I was fortunate to have had him as long as I did. He saw me through the publication of *A Mother and Two Daughters*, which was my first novel to become a bestseller and my third to be a finalist for the National Book Award. He came up with the idea of titling my next book, a novella and five stories, *Mr. Bedford and the Muses* instead of *Mr. Bedford and Five Stories*. He was a man of grace notes. When he had finished reading the manuscript of *The Finishing School*, he put Chopin's Scherzo in B flat Minor on the stereo in his Princeton study, and I could hear its opening bars when I answered my phone in Woodstock. This was the "all clear" scherzo Julian DeVane in *The Finishing School* played to summon his sister, Ursula, back from the fields after he had finished teaching music to children in their house.

Alan was a serious lover of music; he was the first polymath I ever knew well, if anyone could claim to know Alan well. Like some people in the religious life, he could talk engagingly about almost anybody or anything without "getting personal." The only time I ever saw him show emotion was on a windswept night when he was visiting Robert and me in our rented beach cottage on Pawleys Island in the summer of 1985, and he told us, having to steady his face, how the young women from the Olympic hockey team had shown up en masse for the funeral of his aunt Ann, their hockey coach. By that time he had resigned abruptly from Viking after the CEO of Penguin, during the corporate restructuring of Viking, had screamed at him, but Alan was to bestow a magnanimous editorial gift on Robert during that visit with us. Robert had been typing some vignettes of his rich and eventful life, and Alan read them and suggested he break them up into chapters and send what he had to Charles McGrath at the *New Yorker.*

"Once something appears in the *New Yorker*," Alan told Robert, "editors in publishing houses call you up and want to make a contract for a book." This is just what happened. Several months later, when Robert felt they were good enough, he sent some chapters to McGrath and heard back almost immediately. The *New Yorker* wanted to publish Robert's long chapter about his sixteenth year working in wartime Palestine as a traveling accompanist for the old

German tenor Hermann Jadlowker, whom the kaiser had
once called "My Lohengrin" and who had known Brahms.
Here they are in the old Zion Hotel, halfway up Mount
Carmel; for some reason only a single room has been booked
and two single beds have been pushed close together.

It seemed quite unreal that I should be in the same room,
almost in the same bed, with a man who had sung for
Brahms. By now Jadlowker had settled in his bed. "Brahms
had a large pot belly," he said, "and he kept his foot on the
pedal a lot." I had not played much Brahms, but the
thought did occur to me that a protruding belly might
account for why the left and right hand in his piano writing often seemed so far apart . . . I had never heard
Jadlowker talk so much and so freely, and I did not want
him to ever stop talking. Through listening to him I felt
that somehow I knew these men myself—men who until
then had been just names in books and on the title pages
of printed music. I also felt that through having made
music with Jadlowker, I had entered a chain of musical
continuity, and that if someday I was to tell this to someone else, he or she would also become part of it.

McGrath told Robert they would have run all the chapters
if they'd had the space. "I wish everyone wrote as sparsely

and clearly and directly as you," he said. Joe Fox at Random House, tipped off about the *New Yorker* sale by John Irving, asked John Hawkins to see the manuscript and bought it. Robert named it *Continuo*. Shortly after, the English publisher Tom Rosenthal bought it for Andre Deutsch and a portion of it was published in *The Times* of London.

I've always delighted in Virginia Woolf's flat-out assertion (in "Mr. Bennett and Mrs. Brown," her essay about the ways authors present their characters) that "on or about December, 1910, human character changed." In the same spirit, I will likewise declare that on Labor Day weekend, 1983, the publishing business changed for me.

It was Saturday afternoon, September 3, 1983, in Woodstock when I heard the faraway ringing of the kitchen phone. I had turned off my bedroom phone before taking a nap. I had been dreaming of the characters in *The Finishing School*, which was in its final chapters. The phone kept ringing, so I plugged in the bedroom phone and answered.

"Have you heard?" asked John Hawkins.

In the coming years this salutation, delivered in his ominous rumble, was to become so frequent that John took to prefacing it with his special dire chuckle.

"Heard what? It's *Saturday.*"

"On Thursday Peter Mayer walked into Viking and fired the president, Irv Goodman. Nobody's answering their phones over there, but it's rumored there's a bloodbath coming."

Peter Mayer was the CEO of Penguin Books, which had bought Viking Press in 1975; he was also a neighbor of ours, and spent weekends in Woodstock when he was not in London.

I saw gentlemanly Irv Goodman standing on the lovely Persian carpet in front of his desk, only the reds in it were now pools of blood.

"Alan is still there, unless he quits," said John. "I finally reached his assistant at home, but Connie Sayre, the marketing director, was close to Irv, so everyone is worried about her."

"But we were all working so well together! Why does there have to be a bloodbath?"

"Peter said Viking isn't making enough money and Viking and Penguin now answer to Pearson, the multinational book company."

I was within two months of completing *The Finishing School.* Viking was publishing my novella about the young people in the London boardinghouse, *Mr. Bedford and the Muses*, the following week.

After John and I hung up, the phone rang again. It was Peter Mayer's wife, Mary, wondering if we were free for lunch at their Woodstock house tomorrow.

Robert and I were invited for twelve thirty. Knowing the Mayers' laid-back style, we tried our best to be late, but still arrived at twelve forty-five. Peter and two other half-naked men were digging a trench in the private road. Peter, pouring sweat, gleefully informed us that his two assisting ditchdiggers were John Webster, the financial director of Penguin International, and Mr. Blass, the cochairman of Penguin. "Oh, yes," they cried, "we're the slaves!"

Robert and I sort of hung around while the men went back to their digging. Mary came out of the house and asked us if we wanted a drink. Then Peter's former secretary from his days at Pocket Books arrived with her husband. Mary brought our drinks and we sat around the picnic table and swatted off bugs from the pond below. Mary, a new mother, enumerated the advantages of the infant section in British versus American planes. The British had the baby cots at shelf level, while the American ones were on the floor. American planes had infant safety belts attached to the mother's safety belts, whereas on British planes the mother held the baby in her arms. Soon after, Peter's parents, Alfred and Lee Mayer, arrived, and we talked about Woodstock things. Alfred Mayer was the publisher of

Overlook Press, which he and Peter had started together. Alfred had just bought our friend Maria Bauer's Prague memoir, *Beyond the Chestnut Trees*, which he was publishing in the spring of 1984. Maria and Robert Bauer were our close Woodstock friends.

After the sweaty ditchdiggers had showered and dressed, I asked John Webster whether he was a descendant of the John Webster who wrote *The White Devil*. Peter came to his rescue. At last the nutcrackers and picks were laid out and Mary presented us each with a whole lobster accompanied by yellow rice and sliced tomatoes. We began with Folinari wine and then switched to red. I told Mr. Webster, a rugby-ish type from Lincolnshire, how I had traveled in the Midlands and northeast England for the U.S. Travel Service in the 1960s. He said he had been with Price Waterhouse before he came to Penguin.

Peter and I were playing a little game. I was determined to play by social rules and not be the first to mention Viking or the publishing business and not to go within a hundred miles of the subject nearest my heart, the fate of Alan Williams. After Mr. Webster and I had finished discussing what made selling books different from selling fabric or ketchup, I waved my nutcracker at my host. "Now listen, Peter, you must tell me . . ." I said, "how to tackle this lobster."

He said, "Oh!" and laughed. "I thought you were going to ask what I was going to do about Viking."

I didn't rise to the bait, and Peter showed me how to crack the claws and extricate the meat with the pick. When he left the table on some errand, I said to my new friend Mr. Webster, "Tell me, is Viking broke, or what?"

"Oh, no, no! Certainly not. Absolutely not." He launched into corporate assurances to a worried author, and Peter, reappearing promptly, explained how he himself would be staying in New York for the time being to oversee Viking's restructuring.

Mr. Webster told me Peter had a thirty-eight-year-old boss whom neither he nor Peter liked. This boss had asked Peter if he would stay on at Penguin for another five years. But this boss hadn't actually made Peter an offer yet, Mr. Webster confided.

After Peter's father told a story about meeting a bear on two legs while hiking in the mountains around Woodstock, the senior Mayers left for the outdoor concert at the Maverick.

Robert and I stayed a little longer. I helped Mary clear the table, and we all drank more wine. Viking wasn't discussed anymore, and the name of Alan Williams never uttered.

When Robert and I got home, I said: "You know what worries me most about this afternoon? Even the Peter Mayers have to be scared of somebody now."

During Peter's restructuring at Viking, nine more people were fired. One old-school editor, Cork Smith, resigned in "honorable protest" of the firings. Connie Sayre survived the bloodbath and lasted at Viking until 1986. Irv Goodman's successor was a man who had made his name selling toys. Alan Williams, although stripped of his power to authorize substantial advances (under the new regime he wouldn't have been able to authorize the one paid for *A Mother and Two Daughters*) stayed on for a while, during which time he edited *The Finishing School*. However, he had resigned from Viking before that novel was published, in 1985, and Kathryn Court saw it through production and publication. It was on the bestseller list for a number of weeks, and I signed fifteen hundred copies for a Franklin Library first edition. The story of a lonely fourteen-year-old girl and her dramatic and somewhat unstable mentor, it remains a favorite in high school reading courses and book clubs. Peter Mayer eventually stepped down as CEO of Penguin and runs Overlook Press. Overlook's books are now distributed by Penguin, which has merged with Bantam, Dell, Doubleday, Random House, and Knopf to become Penguin Random House. When Robert's health worsened in the mid-1990s and he felt too sad to compose music, he decided to write a novel about an Austrian-born piano teacher, Bernard Winter, who prepares gifted American children for performance. "It is another way

Robert's Yamaha Grand

"When Robert's health worsened . . . and he felt too sad to compose music,
he decided to write a novel about an Austrian-born piano teacher."

my life could have gone," Robert said. He asked Peter Mayer to read it, and Peter liked it and wanted to edit it himself and publish it. In the spring of 1997, Overlook published *The Music Teacher*, with its beautiful cover art of Carnegie Hall from the view of someone on the stage. Robert dedicated the book "to all my friends who teach music." Meanwhile, he was once again writing music.

That 1983 Labor Day weekend was a little drama acted out on the Woodstock stage announcing the next era of publishing. I was to be one of many authors caught in the tumult while it thrashed about in search of a new business model.

Of course publishing had begun to change when I was admitted to its inner sanctum in 1970. Publishing as a family business, as a literate, gentlemanly occupation, had already taken on the sepia hues of nostalgia, but the new publishing, whatever that creature would turn out to be, hadn't reared its head yet. In the meantime, "the industry," as John Hawkins referred to it in his acerbic moods, went through some ungainly and ruthless stages. It still hasn't finished deciding what kind of creature it is supposed to be, and is now circling its wagons to fend off its monster predator, the Internet. Not one of the seven houses that wanted to publish *A Mother and Two Daughters*—eight, counting Knopf, who reserved the right to match the final bidder—stands by itself today. Six of those bidders are now subsumed into two of the "big five" publishing corporations.

Returning for a moment to the dance image that opened this chapter, let's say there has been an intermission, and when we publishing partners (authors, editors, and publishers) return to the dance we notice things are different. A proliferation of nondancers has taken to the floor, wearing in their lapels tiny logos that have nothing to do with publishing. They don't dance but just monitor our movements, like bodyguards with earpieces and dark glasses, only it isn't our bodies they are protecting, it is an unseen corporate body. A mood of foreboding has blighted the air of camaraderie and grace. We sense we are expected to dance faster or more gainfully, and our uncertainty makes us tense. Any one of us could trip, or fall behind, and be tapped on the shoulder by one of the corporate nondancers and asked to leave the floor. Even the floor feels wobbly beneath our feet, and the traditional old building that has supported us has sprung holes in its roof, through which we glimpse patches of an indefinite space in which communications zip back and forth in ways not entirely imaginable to the most far-seeing among us.

Ever since that Labor Day lunch when John Webster, formerly of Price Waterhouse and no relation to the John Webster who wrote *The White Devil*, confided to me that

Peter had not yet had his Penguin contract renewed, I've been uncomfortably aware of what a large role the fear element plays in current publishing. Unless you own your publishing company, however far up you are on the ladder, there's always going to be someone further up who can make you clean out your desk by the end of the workday *and* sign an agreement not to bad-mouth your evictors if you want to receive your severance package. In the following chapters you will get used to John Hawkins telephoning to say, "Have you heard?" Or "Bad news, So-and-so's been fired." And the "so-and-so" will be my editor or my publisher, in some cases both.

It's hard to maintain your equilibrium when your dance partners keep getting dragged off the floor.

This element of fear seeps into all the corridors and crannies of the publishing structure. When I recall those welcoming faces greeting me on my first visit to the Viking headquarters on the last day of 1980, I can't help picturing their counterparts today: still assembled as a united group to welcome a new author but all of them watching their backs, each wondering who among them is the least indispensable.

Publishing Partners, Continued

The big difficulty throughout this projected book will be to know, to learn to know, when I must depart from the literal truth and find the right parallels, the matching fictional realities, the correct inner private symbolisms. Already, just in contemplating the writing of it, I have felt sickened at having to deal with certain realities, tired or bored at the thought of others, and uplifted and intrigued at some others . . . it gives me an opportunity to put more of myself in it than anything else I can imagine. And yet I know the dark days will come when I doubt my right to such an "indulgence." But the way I see it now, it's not an indulgence as much as it is an artistic challenge and an emotional duty.

Spring 1984 notes to myself on beginning
A Southern Family

In the spring of 1985, while *The Finishing School* was still on the hardcover bestseller list and the reviews were still coming in, John Hawkins said it was the right time to go looking for a new contract. By that time I had completed four long chapters of *A Southern Family*, roughly 150 pages of the finished book, which would come to 540 pages in hardcover. That was only 24 pages shorter than the hardcover of *A Mother and Two Daughters* (1982). It would, like *A Mother and Two Daughters*, spend weeks on the *New York Times* bestseller list, though fewer than its predecessor. Of all my books (so far), *A Mother and Two Daughters* has been the only one to achieve the number one fiction spot—in paperback, for a single week until knocked down to number two by Father Andrew Greeley. I consider *A Southern Family* to be the more complex and profound of the two novels, though *A Mother and Two Daughters* is an easier and more engaging read.

A Mother and Two Daughters, based on a best friend's savage anecdotes about a contentious summer trip with her widowed mother and sister, is, in its ultimate resolutions under the umbrella of society, a comedy. *A Southern Family*, based on the 1983 violent deaths of my twenty-eight-year-old half brother and his girlfriend, has a wider sweep of character and social class. It is a tragedy in that nothing is resolved and the social fabric is in tatters. It was, and remains, the most autobiographical of my books and was the most difficult to write. The difficulties didn't arise from problems of composition or incentive: I could hardly stop writing it. There were things that I wanted and needed to find out: Who was this doomed boy with whom I shared a mother? What had all of us left undone that might have saved him?

I looked forward to entering the minds of the characters most alien and unlovable to me and seeing what new perspectives they might bring. (And they certainly delivered those perspectives.) But my difficulties sprang from the ongoing dramas being enacted by the real family as they continued to live their actual lives in the same time frame that I was composing my novel. There was a bitter custody hearing over Tommy's three-year-old son and, following that, a divorce brewing between my mother and stepfather. My mother had more or less anointed me to write this book, something with a beginning and an end that could contain the horror. "*You* will write Tommy's story," she told me the day of his funeral. But, as my chapters were accruing in Woodstock, the animosities between Tommy's father and mother were intensifying in Asheville. My stepfather said if I presented him as a bad person in the novel, he would sue me for everything I had.

After Hawkins told me it was time to seek a new publisher, I revised and polished the first four chapters of *A Southern Family*. (Chapter four, "Magnolia Leaves," was told from the father-stepfather's point of view.) Hawkins made the requisite copies for Viking and two for Avon, the paperback house that had published my last three books and had first refusal rights. Linda Grey, president of Bantam, and Steve Rubin, whom I had met when he interviewed me for his newsletter, *Writers Bloc*, wanted to be in on the bidding if we held an auction. Viking-Penguin had first right of refusal and made a generous offer, but I didn't want to stay with them. Morrow's president, Larry Hughes, and Avon's Rena Wolner bid against Bantam's Linda Grey and Steve Rubin for a two-book contract. After much deliberation I chose Morrow. Harvey Ginsberg, who would be my editor at Morrow, was a known quantity to me; at present he was editing my fellow writers Robb Forman Dew and John Irving. Larry Hughes, back in his own editing days, had seen Paul Scott through his massive Raj Quartet. Larry's astute reading of the first part of *A Southern Family* coupled with his assurances to Hawkins that he would put all Morrow's forces behind the book made me choose Morrow over Bantam.

"*A Southern Family* is all we hoped it would be," Larry generously wrote to me after he and the others in the house had read the final manuscript. A seasoned publisher, he knew what it took to give a book a propitious send off. At the American Booksellers Association meeting in Washington, D.C. in the spring of 1987, he held a dinner at the Willard Hotel in my honor for the major book critics. He arranged for me to speak to booksellers at the ABA breakfast. *A Southern Family* was my first Book-of-the-Month Club main selection and would get my first front-page review in the *New York Times Book Review*. Larry retired before *A Southern Family* was published, in the fall of 1987, but all the important groundwork had been laid.

However, the new publishing ethos was firmly in place by 1990, when I turned in the second novel of the two-book contract with Morrow, and it made itself felt right from the start. The entire contractually allowed month of silence passed before John Hawkins received word that Morrow-Avon had accepted the manuscript of *Father Melancholy's Daughter*. Soon afterward, Hawkins reported to me the behind-doors story, courtesy of Harvey Ginsberg. "There is no way I can earn back the advance on this book," Carolyn Reidy, now president of Avon, had told the new Morrow president, Howard Kaminsky. Reidy advised the team to turn it down. She and Kaminsky were leaning toward rejection when Al Marciano, the company treasurer, asked if it was a matter of the book's quality. Oh no, he was told, it might even be her best book, quality-wise, but in subject matter it wasn't as saleable as *A Southern Family*. "Well, then," Marciano said, "aren't we obliged to honor our commitment?" In that instance the old-school team member prevailed and the acceptance check was issued.

The battle continued, however. Kaminsky phoned Hawkins to say: "Her title just doesn't shout big book." Also the team felt *Father Melancholy's Daughter* had too many syllables. ("See if you can get her to change it.") Embattled, I lay awake compiling an arsenal of multisyllabic titles of "big books" for John to pummel Kaminsky with: *The Brothers Karamazov, Sense and Sensibility, The Prime of Miss Jean Brodie, Dinner at the Homesick Restaurant, The World According to Garp, A La Recherche du Temps Perdu.*

Meanwhile, attacks had begun on another flank. Carolyn Reidy thought the novel was too long; it took too much time getting to the love interest, the meeting of Margaret and Adrian, halfway through. There was a new system in place at Morrow-Avon, John was informed, in which the hardcover editor and the paperback editor *shared their editing suggestions* with the author. My hardcover editor, Harvey Ginsberg, called to tell me Judith Riven, the paperback editor, would be sending me, separately, her suggestions for cuts. In a conspiratorial sotto voce he added: "But don't do anything you don't feel like doing."

Father Melancholy's Daughter kept its title, but I did end up cutting about ten thousand words at Judith's suggestion. Do I regret it? Yes. Some good material was lost. But at the time I felt uncertain and kept second-guessing myself: do I really need this . . . and this? The cut version in book form came to 404 pages, 160 pages shorter than *A Mother and Two Daughters*, and 136 pages shorter than *A Southern Family*. *Father Melancholy's Daughter* was a Book-of-the-Month Club main selection and a Franklin Library signed first edition, and it appeared in the number twelve spot on the *Times* bestseller list for one week. For my interview with the *Today* show's Katie Couric, I was flown to Washington at the last minute because she had to be there to meet General Norman Schwarzkopf on his return from the Gulf War.

Because of the contract for *A Southern Family* and *Father Melancholy's Daughter*, I was able to take two huge steps that enhanced my life and the lives of the two people closest to me. Robert and I built the Woodstock house, in which I still live, and we enjoyed it together for fourteen years. He called it, depending on his mood, the Factory, the Orphanage, or Villa Godstar. He wrote music on his last day in this house, a song called "Evening." We moved into Villa Godstar on July 1, 1987, three months before *A Southern Family* was published.

In early January 1987, I was able to buy a beautiful condo in Asheville for my mother when she decided to end a marriage of thirty-nine years and live alone for the first time in her life, at the age of seventy-five. She had gone straight from home to college to a brief marriage, followed by ten years of supporting her widowed mother and small child by

Villa Godstar

Gail and Robert's Woodstock house.

writing and teaching, then into a second marriage and three more children: Franchelle Cole Millender, now an attorney; the late Tommy Cole, who will always be an enigma; and her youngest, Rebel Cole, now a professor of finance. She had never slept in a house by herself until she lay down in her new bed at 1902 Timber Trail, which looked out at the mountains. Here she lived among things she had chosen, preferring clean spaces to objects she didn't want to look at; she ate what she liked (oatmeal, grapes, Lean Cuisine, and chocolate) and lost thirty pounds; she slept when she pleased, or not at all. After a lifetime of concealing her privacy behind an illegible script, she took a course in calligraphy, and set out to write a daily chronicle of her new life in spiral notebooks that anyone could read. Gifted at needlework, she sewed and embroidered silk cases for the notebooks. She mailed them to me as she wrote them—just as she used to let me read her stories and novels as they came out of the typewriter. "Would you consider letting me put these in my Wilson Library archives at Chapel Hill?" I asked. "I mean, after we are both dead, of course." "Better not wait for *both* of us to be dead before you put them in," she suggested with her old wicked smile.

Her journals reveal a woman disciplined in the skills of writing, living fully in the midst of her times, and determined to be accountable. She writes about becoming a

Kathleen's journals
"Would you consider letting me put these in my
Wilson Library archives at Chapel Hill?"

Helpmate, on call for battered women—"If I managed to leave, at my age," she told them at secret meeting spots, "you can do it, too." She hammered home her point in domiciliary care meetings ("old people still have bodies") until she got exercise programs started in nursing homes, and she taught an overflowing course in Asheville history at the local university. Reviewing her past life, she saw new angles of it, some humiliating, some fortunate, some devastating. Occasionally she would write, "This is all I can take now—will try to go on with it some other time." Faithfully chronicling until the day before her death, she reported how worthy projects finally got accomplished in tiresome committee meetings and often what strangers said to her on the street. To a young man complaining that the library was closed, she gave the reminder that today was King's birthday. "Oh!" he cried happily. "And here I didn't even know it was Stephen King's birthday!"

A Southern Family and *Father Melancholy's Daughter* did not earn out the advance by a long shot, but before *Father Melancholy* was published in 1991, John had signed me for a two-book contract with Random House–Ballantine. Even before the auction between the Book-of-the-Month Club and the Literary Guild had taken place, and long before the starred reviews of *Father Melancholy's Daughter* appeared in *Publishers Weekly* and *Kirkus*, John had approached Howard Kaminsky about a new contract for my next two novels. I don't know what was said, because all I recorded in my journal at the time was that "Kaminsky really hurt John's feelings" on Monday. By Thursday of the same week John had got opening bids from Bob Wyatt, who was now at Ballantine with Susan Petersen, and from Steve Rubin and Linda Grey at Doubleday-Bantam.

The two works named in the new contract up for bidding were *My Last Protégé* and *The Very Rich Hours of Freddy Stratton.* By the time of signing, I had written several chapters and an outline of the first novel and a plot summary of the second. (Though neither of these novels ever came into being, parts of them were to find their way into future novels.)

That 1990 auction, won by Susan Petersen and Bob Wyatt at Ballantine, would mark the peak of my desirability status in the publishing industry. Never again would publishers bid so much and so wildly for the honor of having me on their list. "This is getting crazy, don't you think?" I said to Hawkins during the auction. "No," he said, "both houses want you because you'd be the literary plum on their list, and because *A Mother and Two Daughters* has sold over a million copies and goes on selling, and they also want you to keep their competitors from getting you."

I was visiting Asheville when the bidding reached its culmination. It had been going on all morning when Susan Petersen phoned me herself to say, "Please come with us. I feel like I'm asking you to marry me." Though her recklessness charmed me, I explained I had to get off the phone now, because I was already late to pick up a nun I was taking on a picnic. "Oh, God," she cried, "that is right out of one of your novels." I think that is what did it for me: *A Southern Family* had ended with a picnic on the mountain with a nun.

I drove across town to the convent, having promised John Hawkins to phone him collect before going out of reach on the picnic. And in a tiny parlor I made the call to New York from an old-model telephone I recognized from the "telephone closet" of the now-torn-down Victorian structure where I had gone to school in the forties and fifties. Then away I went on the picnic with Sister Winters, with whom I had been close ever since she was my eighth-grade teacher. It was raining, so we sat under the eaves of a little church on top of a mountain. I remember saying something like "I can't believe how much money they're going to give me," and I remember her saying she was glad, and then we ate our fried chicken thighs and celery sticks and hard-boiled eggs, and drank our bottle of red wine and talked of other things.

When Hawkins was finalizing the 1990 Random House–Ballantine contract, he was still raw from Kaminsky and

Auction Day, 1990

"It was raining, so we sat under the eaves of a
little church on top of a mountain."

Reidy's attempted jettisoning of *Father Melancholy's Daughter.* He and Susan Petersen and Bob Wyatt drafted a new rider that would squash any such attempt in the future. Though the final version of this rider got modified, I photo-copied that first draft and have kept it in my desk drawer. I like to check myself off against its lofty expectations.

> In evaluating whether the complete manuscript is satis-factory, the Publisher may consider only (i) whether, in the opinion of the Publisher's counsel, it violates the copy-right, right or privacy or any other right of any person or contains libelous or obscene matter, and (ii) its conformity with the length requirements of Rider to Paragraph 1 hereof and with the professional and literary standards exemplified by A SOUTHERN FAMILY. "Professional and literary standards" include such factors as writing style, accuracy, originality, clarity, grammar, organization, realism, plot development, character development, cred-ibility, intellectual and emotional appeal and geographic and temporal sweep.

Susan Petersen was still president of Ballantine when I abandoned the ninety pages of *My Last Protégé*, a novel told from the viewpoint of Augusta (Gus), an architect, who meets her high school protégé twenty years later at a mutual friend's funeral. In high school Edmund was a withdrawn, fat boy with no social skills until Gus took him in hand and transformed him into a handsome and mysterious creature everybody wanted. Now he has returned to town, more attractive and mysterious than ever, with an older man and a shy, almost feral, young girl, and all three are going to live in Edmund's old family house. And then, on page 90, as a plague of locusts descends on Gus and Edmund's town, and Gus realizes she is in love with her old protégé, the novel simply died. This happens. It happened with *The Angel Keeper*, also on page 90. These deaths hurt. But dead is dead.

My Last Protégé was to have been about new beginnings and unexpected choices. *The Good Husband*, the novel that replaced it, was about dying and reviewing your old choices. In retrospect I see how in the early 1990s death had become my abiding interest. Robert had recently learned that he had multiple myeloma, a cancer of the bone marrow, and congestive heart failure. One or the other was going to take him out. ("Each year I could do less and less," he was to tell the nurse who was with him at his death.) Of all subjects, how a person prepared for death was the one closest to my heart.

I had written about a third of *The Good Husband*, which divides points of view among Magda Danvers, a dying academic who looks upon meeting death as her "final exam;"

Francis Lake, her devoted, younger househusband; Hugo Henry, an irascible writer; and Alice, his young wife, unsteady from a history of mental illness and the recent loss of their child. I took a photo of the different colored chapter folders spread out on a hassock and mailed it to Susan to show her I was making progress.

Soon after, the gift of a beautiful white blanket arrived with a warm note from Susan, but the next thing I knew my phone was ringing. "Bad news," said Hawkins, "Susan's out." I was left high and dry as my editor-to-be, Bob Wyatt, had left Ballantine some months before. Later John phoned with news of Susan's successor at Ballantine: Linda Grey, who with Steve Rubin at Bantam had lost out on the two previous auctions for my books! I have given Linda her own chapter in this book, "The Wings of the Dove." She was truly a casualty of the new publishing ethos.

In *Evensong*, the novel that eventually got written instead of *The Very Rich Hours of Freddy Stratton*, Augusta (Gus), the architect from *My Last Protégé*, who is now my new protagonist's best friend, finally gets her story told. The mystery of the new Edmund is also revealed.

Further down the line, into another era of contracts, Freddy Stratton would shape-shift into Tildy Stratton of *Unfinished Desires*, the queen bee at her girls' school. *The Very Rich Hours* was to have had this convent school as its background; its tragedy was to have been that, for Freddy, her high school beauty and popularity represented the peak of her life. It was all downhill afterward. The present time of *The Very Rich Hours* was Freddy's fiftieth year, when she is dying. In *Unfinished Desires*, largely set during Tildy's ninth-grade year, Tildy, far from a beauty but an inspired troublemaker, shares the stage with several other major characters and the time span begins with the founding of the school in 1908 and takes Tildy's ninth-grade class into their fifties.

Sometimes plans that you think went up in smoke will materialize at a later date and fit perfectly into a new work.

The Good Husband, published in 1994, remains my favorite failure. I don't mean an artistic failure—I can still leaf through its pages and get a jolt of artistic sustenance—but a public failure, a *publishing failure*. "The book sold only 30,000 copies," I confided in shame to my journal, though in retrospect thirty thousand doesn't seem all that bad.

The Good Husband disappointed many people on many counts: its reception disappointed Linda Grey, my publisher. Despite her sending me on two coast-to-coast book tours, the book came nowhere near to making "the list." It infuriated or irritated reviewers in key places who claimed that I had "attempted too much" or that "the characters were unlovable." ("I just wanted to smack Alice down," a TV

hostess in Denver crowed exultantly to me on her show.)
Devotees of *Father Melancholy's Daughter* had been hoping
for another character like Margaret, the dedicated daughter
on the path to her own ministry. They had wanted to *be*
Margaret. I received letters from women who said they
were seeking ordination because of Margaret's story.
Whereas there was not one among the four protagonists in
The Good Husband that a reader would gladly "identify
with." The most colorful and gifted one, the teacher Magda,
is dying of cancer. The three others are bogged down in
personal failures and losses. Yet the sheer life of all of them
as they go about figuring out how to right themselves contin-
ues to amaze me. Though they started off as parts of me or
of people I thought I knew, they add up to more than the
sum of us. Even though I wrote it, it is one of those novels
from which I continue to glean wisdom, as when Magda, in
a dying dream, stands in front of her students with her guts
falling out and tells them the reason she can see straight
through people now is because *she doesn't want anything
from them anymore.*

The final book of the Ballantine contract made with Susan
Petersen, the novel that got written instead of *The Very Rich
Hours of Freddy Stratton*, turned out to be an unplanned
sequel to *Father Melancholy's Daughter. Evensong* was the
story of Margaret's ministry and her marriage, set in the last

year of the twentieth century. There was a five-year gap between *The Good Husband* (1994) and *Evensong* (1999), and John Hawkins had to ask Linda Grey to extend the contract deadline for Work Number 2.

Evensong was a critical success and made a one-week appearance (number 12) on the *Times* list. It is still taught in seminaries and is a favorite on Lenten reading lists. After its publication, General Theological Seminary awarded me an honorary doctorate of divinity. The original painting of a nighttime village in the mountains that Linda Grey commissioned for the book jacket hangs in a cherished place in my study. The novel, my tenth, did not come anywhere close to earning out its advance.

So I was flabbergasted when in 2002 Random House–Ballantine made an enthusiastic offer for a short (114 pages) fictional memoir, *Evenings at Five*, which included twenty drawings. "Why?" I asked John Hawkins. "When my bottom line at Ballantine has been in parentheses for years."

John explained that (a) they wanted to keep their option on the next big fiction contract, and (b) Nancy Miller, Ballantine's new editor in chief, was excited about it. When John was offering it around, Nancy had called and said, "John, I want this. What are the rules?" "The rule is love," John told her. Nancy would have jumped in her car and driven up to Woodstock immediately and told me in person of her love had it not been for an event at her youngest son's school.

Evenings at Five was an act of love and grief, written on consecutive evenings in the year following Robert's death in April 2001. It was a celebration of him and our life together for almost thirty years, of the house we had built, of his wit and his rages, of his swift and alarming physical decline, and, not least of all, of our cocktail hours together. My original title for it was *The Pope Called*, which was Robert's statement to signal me it was time to stop our work for the day and meet downstairs for that first cocktail.

My friend Frances Halsband, who drew the illustrations for this book, did the pen-and-ink drawings: exteriors and interiors of the house; Robert's medicine shelves, which I had not yet dismantled; Robert's work desk and piano; my work desk; Robert's Stickley chair and Turkish cushion; a favorite kitchen knife; an etched cocktail glass given to him on a houseboat in wartime Cairo.

I had met Frances Halsband in 1990, when I thought I was going to be writing *My Last Protégé*, the novel about the architect. I had asked Beverly Russell, who edited an architecture magazine, to find me such a woman at the top of her game. At the lunch date Beverly set up for us at a Woodstock restaurant, Frances and I quickly realized we had years of intimate conversations ahead of us. Each of us was fascinated by the nuts and bolts of the other's work and by certain dramatic contrasts: if Frances erred in her vision of a work, millions of dollars could be lost or a structure could collapse, whereas I could just wipe the slate of my mind clean and start over. We laughed a lot about this. We also had many "professional women anecdotes" to laugh about. When she was elected the first woman president of the American Institute of Architects, the man who introduced her started off by praising her legs; when I turned in my novel about a female academic, the editor said I hadn't mentioned whether she wanted children and I needed to clarify her feelings about this for my readers. Frances was married to another Robert (the architect Robert Kliment), who, like my Robert, had been born in Europe and had grown up in other countries during World War Two. They had a weekend house in Woodstock, and the four of us became friends.

Frances received 15 percent of the *Evenings at Five* advance for her exquisite drawings, and we had a joint book signing at a Barnes & Noble store in midtown Manhattan. John Hawkins threw a book party for us at his apartment, which he later asked Frances to redesign for him.

In May 2013, when I had one chapter left to write for *Publishing*, I was laying out my book tour clothes for my novel *Flora* on the bed and suddenly wished Frances could draw the scene as I saw it: the svelte new carry-on "spinner"

Packing for book tour

Silver jacket, Victorian brooch, and "silver eminence" beads.

suitcase, the twenty-four-year-old silver Armani jacket, the Victorian brooch and strapped evening shoes. The objects were all but animate in their statement about the "author performances" that usually accompany a book's publication. I asked Frances if she was willing to read the chapters and consider doing her pen-and-ink drawings of certain objects and places for a new book I was writing about publishing. She leapt on board and surpassed herself, flying to Chapel Hill and drawing the significant buildings, visiting my archives at the Wilson Library (the star in the upper-right-hand corner of that drawing had to be stamped on her drawing paper to show she wasn't sneaking out any papers from the archive). She took the train to Washington to draw the Lehrers' drawing room and library, which held the party at the end of this book.

Nancy Miller did come to see me in Woodstock after becoming my editor at Ballantine, arriving in the first hybrid car I had ever seen. Here was another professional woman at the top of her game with whom I had immediate rapport. I entrusted her with two folders of work in progress: the opening chapters of *Queen of the Underworld* and the first year of my apprentice journals from 1962–1969, which Rob Neufeld, the book critic of the *Asheville Citizen-Times*, was editing and footnoting for me. Her response to the novel was quick and passionate. She loved Emma Gant, the ferociously ambitious young reporter set loose in the Miami of 1959. She also wanted to publish the journals.

Hawkins negotiated the four-book contract (two volumes of journals, *Queen of the Underworld*, and a second novel, to be called *The Red Nun*) with Gina Centrello, the president of Ballantine. (A year later Gina would become head of the newly merged Random House–Ballantine, Nancy Miller would move with her, and these four books would be published under the Random House imprint.)

Queen of the Underworld (2006) did not make any best-seller lists, though it has since become the "problem child" favorite of all my works. I named its protagonist Emma Gant—the Gant after Thomas Wolfe's voraciously ambitious Eugene Gant, the Emma after Jane Austen's eponymous protagonist, about whom Austen said when beginning her novel: "I am going to take a heroine whom no one but myself will much like."

We meet Emma Gant as she boards the train for her Miami newspaper job the same day she graduates from journalism school. Her go-getterism was too much for some readers: "Get over yourself!" was the headline of the *USA Today* review. Though Emma had her champions, too. The National Public Radio critic Alan Cheuse wrote: "You would think that by this time America might have produced a dramatic and moving bildungsroman about a female writer in her formative years . . . finally we have a book that more than fills the role: Gail Godwin's *Queen of the Underworld*."

At the start of the novel, I resolved not to have an older, mellower Emma looking back on her embarrassingly vainglorious young self who was hell-bent on making it as a top journalist, famous novelist, and femme fatale—all three as soon as possible. No, I would stay right inside young Emma and we would do our worst together. Nancy Miller stabilized me in this resolve. At one point I said, "Oh, God, maybe I should skip over Emma's next days and take up the story after she is exiled from Miami to the sleepy Broward bureau and begins to reflect on her actions." "No," said Nancy, "I want to follow her minute by minute through every one of those actions." The entire novel takes place in ten days in June 1959 in Miami. Emma's hotel is filling with Cuban refugees fleeing Castro's new regime. Both Emma and the city are on the cusp of change.

My literary emboldener for *Queen of the Underworld* was Thomas Mann's *Confessions of Felix Krull, Confidence Man: The Early Years*. (There was to be a second volume, but Mann did not live to write it.) Both Felix and Emma know how to beguile, and both began their careers by waiting tables. At last, in this twelfth novel, published in 2006, I was able to bring life to some of the success-hunger I had hoped to capture in the novel I had abandoned in 1958 after the Knopf scout turned down the first five pages of *Windy Peaks.*

Nancy Miller had joined a growing list of Random House's departures by the time I was in the very early stages of *The Red Nun.* I was assigned a new editor whose name I wasn't familiar with. After I looked up the books on her list, I decided we wouldn't suit each other. "Can you rescue me?" I asked John Hawkins.

"Let me ask around over there," he said.

In doing so, he discovered that Jennifer Hershey, with whom I had worked on my nonfiction book *Heart: A Personal Journey Through Its Myths and Meanings* (2001) for Morrow, was now an editor at Random House. She read the chapters John sent her of *The Red Nun* and told him, "We can publish this quite well." So we decided to finish out the contract with Random House since Jennifer would be chaperoning this remaining novel and volume two of *The Making of a Writer.*

After all, she had seen me through *Heart* after my editor for that book was fired.

Heart had been the brainchild of a young editor, Hamilton Cain, who had just been hired by Morrow. He pitched his idea after I had finished *Evensong,* and I thought it would be refreshing to try a book of nonfiction. I estimated the project would take me a year, but those turned out to be the final years of Robert's illness and it took two years. Hamilton Cain was long gone by then, and Jennifer Hershey, who had taught him how to do a profit and loss statement for *Heart*, edited the book. It was published on Valentine's Day, two months before Robert's death. Jennifer came to Robert's funeral in Woodstock with John Hawkins, and this thoughtful act also counted with me in deciding to stay with Random House.

My disappointments concerning the production of *The Red Nun*, aka *Unfinished Desires*, are told in the chapter "The Good Husband, the Sorrowful Mother, and the Red Nun," but I will just add here what is obvious: that the books of authors who haven't earned out their advances for previous books are published under a rain cloud. The publisher's goal by then is to stop the spending, not to "throw more good money after bad," and so there can be no ads, no marketing budget, no enthusiastic gymnastics performed by the publicity department. When I was under my rain cloud with Linda Grey and she said she could not spend any more money, John and I returned a part of my advance to be used for promotion and ads for *Evensong*; we also gave back the foreign rights. I hired Goldberg & McDuffie to take complete charge of the publicity for that book. I hired Camille McDuffie for *Heart* in 2001 and for a third time in 2006 for

Random House's publication of *Queen of the Underworld* and volume one of *The Making of a Writer.* For those two books, published simultaneously, I also paid for ads, designed by Random House, to run in the *New York Times Book Review* and the *New Yorker.* By plowing back my profits from gainful days into a new venture I felt I was behaving like any small business owner who intends to stay in business.

Unfinished Desires was published to good reviews in December 2009, and volume 2 of *The Making of a Writer* came out in January 2011. It was also to receive a positive reception, but by then my standing with Random House had cratered. Jennifer Hershey had become editor in chief of the company's Ballantine imprint.

Since I knew there would be no ads, I decided to write a short essay that I hoped the *New York Times Book Review* would publish as an endpiece around the time of publication of volume 2 of *Making of a Writer*. I wrote about what it was like to be a writer for many years, how what you want from writing changes with age. I wrote about the style and tempo changes of your work habits, and how you look forward to using up your life's materials "like biscuit dough, pushing the leftovers into another and another artful shape— down to the last strange little animal." I called it "The Old Writer," though the book review retitled it "Working on the

Ending." It was published a few weeks before volume 2 of *The Making of a Writer*, and in the little author slot at the bottom of the page was my small proactive "ad" announcing the forthcoming work.

In late November 2011, John Hawkins shocked us all by dying, apparently during an afternoon nap, after a long convalescence from his back and knee surgeries. Friends and clients were dismayed: he had been planning a spring trip to Paris, the city of his youth, to celebrate his recuperation. The last conversation I had with him was on an autumn afternoon when he phoned to tell me how much he loved following an orchestral score on his lap while listening to his iPod. "Robert knew this satisfaction," he said, then reminisced about his years training to be a lyric tenor in Paris.

John's memorial reception was held in early December in the imposing Masonic Hall of the Grand Lodge building on West Twenty-third Street, where John Hawkins and Associates had sixteenth-floor offices. Moses Cardona, John's appointed successor, had put up a display of photos on a table, and here I found myself head to head with someone else gazing on a youthful self. It just happened to be an old photo of the two of us, head to head at a dinner party at his and Cynthia's apartment in the 1980s.

Grand Masonic Hall

"I love it that the setting for this freemasonry among people of the
book was the Grand Masonic Hall in New York on the night we were
celebrating the life of my agent and confidant of forty-three years."

"Weren't we cute?" he said. "Look at all our hair!"

It was Steve Rubin, president and publisher of Henry Holt. We had not been in touch since he and Linda Grey at Bantam had lost the auction to Morrow for *A Southern Family*. I was surprised that Steve would even speak to me, yet we were to spend much of the evening together catching up on publishing and personal lives (we had both lost our partners) and discussing books. He now published Hilary Mantel. He told me he was going home to watch *House of Cards* (the English one) again on DVD, and when I got home to Woodstock I watched it again, too, and thought of Steve.

Just before Christmas, I answered the phone. "This is a voice from the past," said Nancy Miller, who had left Random House when I was in the middle of writing *The Red Nun*. She had been spun around in the great publishing maelstrom herself but recently had become the editorial director of Bloomsbury USA. She had run into Steve Rubin, who told her, "You should call Gail, she's about to finish a book and wants a new publisher."

The book was *Flora*, my fourteenth novel, which I have given a chapter of its own because it represents a new beginning.

"Can I read it? Can I buy it?" asked Nancy, with the playful élan I had so missed.

Of course, Random House had first right of refusal, and they did make a good offer. Moses Cardona and I told them we wanted to start on a new page, and I received a warm note from Jennifer Hershey, who said she understood and that she would keep an eye on my backlist with them.

This brings the dance chronicle up to date. I love it that the setting for this freemasonry among people of the book was the grand Masonic Hall in New York on the night we were celebrating the life of my agent and confidant of forty-three years.

The Wings of the Dove

THE LIFE AND DEATH OF A PUBLISHER

She waited, Kate Croy, for her father to come in . . .
—Henry James, *The Wings of the Dove* (1902)

Whenever I reread that strenuous novel, I always pause during its opening sentence (which goes on for a while longer) and remember Linda Grey, my publisher and editor at Ballantine Books from 1992 until 1999: six years, in all, which represents about one seventh of my years as a published writer to date.

We met for our last dinner on a rainy January evening in 1998 in Manhattan, to celebrate my completion of *Evensong*, the final novel of a two-book contract with Ballantine, a part of the Random House group. It was a low-key, dutiful evening—for both of us, I think, except for the unforgettable personal story she told me.

While the story Linda told me about herself that night was to compress itself over the years into a perfect little horror story of thwarted vocation, the rest of our dinner dissolves into a few dreary memory wisps. We had been given a large room to ourselves because of Linda's chain smoking. We sat side by side on a banquette with the table in front of us. The overhead lighting was too strong for flattery or illusions on either side. Linda had walked from work and I had walked from my hotel. Both of us were tired and trying to cover it up.

Last night, when I had to resort to past diaries, those regulators of misremembering, to help me substantiate this piece of writing, I was astonished how much I had forgotten of the depressing backstory leading up to that dinner.

Linda had inherited me when she moved from Bantam Doubleday Dell to take over Ballantine. This required some good sportsmanship on her part. In her previous job as publisher and editor in chief at Bantam, she had twice been the losing bidder, with Steve Rubin, for two-book contracts for my novels. Now she had become president and publisher of Ballantine, and there I was waiting for her, along with the two books Susan Petersen had won away from her! Nevertheless, Linda told Hawkins that she would like to be my editor as well as my publisher. ("I trained to be an English teacher, you know, John.") Except for one fumble early on, which I will describe in the next chapter, she was a meticulous and caring editor.

In her role as my publisher, she sent me on *two* coast-to-coast book tours, one in the spring before the publication of *The Good Husband* (1994) and the second to coincide with the book's fall publication. The first tour was to, as Linda put it, "reacquaint you with booksellers from Atlanta to San Francisco." My last novel had come out as recently as 1991, which I didn't feel was exactly the distant past, but maybe the publishing powers, ratcheting up everything in order to keep abreast of the spinning world, had decided that readers were getting more impatient. The second tour was to assure this book would make the bestseller list, as had my previous four novels, and earn back the advance her predecessor had paid. Linda herself accompanied me on the bookseller tour and sent her second in command with me for the publication tour. No expenses were spared. (I have yet to meet the equal of that bathroom and shower at the Peninsula Beverly Hills.) The novel got some negative reviews and did not make "the list," though the next one, *Evensong* (1999) did. But by the time that second book was finished Random House had been bought by the German company Bertelsmann, and Linda wrote a formal letter to my agent saying that, alas, my two-book contract was not going to earn out and she could spend no more money on marketing *Evensong*.

Rather than see my stock plummet further, my agent and I offered to give back foreign rights to Random House and forfeit some of my advance in return for ads and promotion that we would specify. I also hired my own publicity firm. *Evensong* was scheduled for publication the following spring. Linda believed in *Evensong*'s story, even though, from a marketing point of view, "religious angles can be tricky." She believed in the characters, that is, after she had convinced me to make Margaret's husband less "passive-aggressive." She commissioned a young painter to do the jacket art, which was to be a rendering of the tiny mountain town where Margaret is a pastor. ("I want the feel of Van Gogh's *Starry Night*, but I want the village to have a Southern mountains look.")

This was how things stood with us the night of the dinner. I don't remember us talking about *Evensong*, maybe we'd already said everything we needed to say over the phone and in letters and faxes, but the forgotten topics I found in the diary were as follows:

A Random House novelist who had combatively corrected her at a recent gathering: "No, there are *three* great American writers: Bellow, Roth . . . and *me.*"

The "vile tantrum" of another Random House novelist whose bound galleys had failed to arrive at a Southern booksellers convention.

Anne Tyler's and Jane Smiley's "wonderful new novels."
(Even the best-meaning publishers can't resist going on a
bit about the other writers on their lists, but I didn't want
to hear it.)

Then came Linda's harrowing *Wings of the Dove* story, which
I remembered without any recourse to a diary.

When she was walking me back to my hotel she asked if I
had started writing a new book and I said, "Yes, but it will
probably make someone jump out the window." "Oh, no,"
she wailed, "that means me." "No, not you," I judiciously
answered, though I assumed it would be. I didn't get very far
with that novel about an order of nuns who host retreats in a
woodland convent near Washington, D.C., and the cross
section of seekers during a period of two weeks—in other
words, *more* religion for poor Linda. As it turned out, we
were never to see each other again.

"The publishing industry is becoming downright hazard-
ous to humans," John Hawkins had commented when
Linda's predecessor, who had so ardently wooed me,
underwent grueling health and personal crises soon
after being fired (though eventually her star would rise
even higher).

What was the new publisher and president like, I asked John. Who *was* Linda Grey? Well, she had risen from the bottom in the industry. Attractive, friendly, but very private. No rumor of any significant other in her life. She lived alone in a modest New York apartment until the huge salary heaped on her by Random House when she became president and publisher of Ballantine impelled her to buy a house in the Hamptons "for an investment" to which she dutifully drove on bumper-to-bumper weekends in the Lexus that Random House leased for her. It had a state-of-the-art kitchen, which she never used. She seldom cooked, except for close friends in the city, and she had no animals or plants.

When I met her I was surprised at how pretty she was: slim, pale, tallish, with blue-gray eyes, short dark curls, and a ret-roussé nose. Her smile had a winning "just between us" intimacy to it. Though not superstylish, she dressed well, except for the scratched brown purse she always lugged over her shoulder.

The night of our last dinner, she told me that her ambition since childhood had been to teach high school English. She went straight from graduation at SUNY Binghamton to Yale, where she had won a scholarship to summer school. For postgraduate credits, she was to teach three remedial sections of high school English and take one intensive course in literature. The single book to be studied in this course was Henry James's late masterpiece, *The Wings of the Dove.*

The high school remedial classes were exhausting and she felt intimidated by Yale. When at last she sat down to apply herself to *The Wings of the Dove*, she entered a living nightmare. The words on the page refused to sustain a narrative. She said it was like *unlearning* to read, going backwards from accumulated meaning to isolated signifiers. She had read and taught other works by James and told herself it was because she was tired, it would be better tomorrow. But it only got worse: the book closed its doors against her like an esoteric club. Eventually she broke down, abandoned her scholarship, and went home to Brooklyn, where her father refused to speak to her for the rest of the summer. She taught English for a while in a very rough high school in Brooklyn, broke down again, then decided to enter publishing. Editorial assistant. Managing editor. Editor in chief. President and publisher.

Evensong was published in March 1999. Linda and I were to meet for an early dinner after I taped *Fresh Air* with Terry Gross. Linda was going to present me with the framed painting she had commissioned for the book jacket. When I got back to my hotel room after the taping, my phone was flashing. Call John Hawkins. "Bad news. Linda's been fired. Thank God this didn't happen two weeks ago or we'd really be up shit creek."

Linda called me from her house in Hampton Bays. Her feelings were hurt, she said, but she considered it a blessing. The stress had been too high. "There is no graciousness in publishing anymore," she said. When she had asked to buy the Lexus they had leased for her, the business office would accept a cashier's check only. "Here I have been in charge of their business for six years and they don't trust my personal check." What she minded most was that she cared about all those people who worked for her. However, everything was in place for *Evensong*. The ads (paid for by me) had been sent out. Fifty thousand copies shipped, second printing ordered. And she would be mailing the painting to me.

This appeared a year and a half later on the *New York Times* obituary page.

September 13, 2000
Linda Grey, 54, a Publisher Who Led the Ballantine Group
By Doreen Carvajal

Linda Grey, a top publishing executive who rose from editorial assistant to president and publisher of the

Ballantine Publishing Group, died on Aug. 30. She was 54 and lived in New York.

The cause was complications from lung cancer, said Alan Davies, a friend of Ms. Grey's.

Ms. Grey resigned from her position at Ballantine last February during a reorganization of the company that came more than a year after the media conglomerate Bertelsmann moved to acquire Ballantine's parent, Random House.

She got her start in publishing in 1970 as an editorial assistant at Coward McCann & Geoghegan. Later she rose to become managing editor there and then took executive positions at Dell Publishing Company, where she was its editor in chief. In 1981 she moved to Bantam Books as an editorial director and became its publisher and editor in chief in 1985.

She left that position in 1992 to start her own short-lived imprint for the company, Linda Grey Books, which published just one book, "It Doesn't Take a Hero: The Autobiography of General Norman H. Schwarzkopf." The imprint was dissolved the same year after the announcement that Ms. Grey was resigning to become president and publisher of the Ballantine Publishing Group . . .

After her resignation from the Ballantine Publishing Group, Ms. Grey, who was unmarried, essentially retired from the publishing industry, although she continued to counsel authors who were her close friends.

They were practically united and splendidly strong; but there were other things—things they were precisely strong enough to be able successfully to count with and safely to allow for; in consequence of which they would for the present, subject to some better reason, keep their understanding to themselves.

Sometimes, when James is being really maddening in *The Wings of the Dove*, I pause at the end of a labyrinthine passage and speak to the exhausted young Linda in summer school at Yale. ("Okay, all that is happening here is Kate and Densher have engaged themselves, but for money reasons they have decided to keep it a secret.")

Then I wonder if she got that far. It's on page 118, after all. What a prose thicket to confront after a day of teaching remedial English! Didn't anyone look over her schedule and suggest maybe—? Or was there a sadistic winnowing process going on here? I can't ask her now, but whenever I reread that novel—and it does offer its abstruse glories and intricate moral windings when you have all the time in the world and no career to make—she's with me.

The Good Husband, The Sorrowful Mother, and The Red Nun

"We reserve to ourselves the right to give another title to the book, for we do not like that of 'The Archer of Charles IX.;' it does not sufficiently excite the curiosity of readers; there are several kings named Charles; and in the middle ages there were great numbers of archers. Now, if you had made it 'The Soldier of Napoleon,' well and good; but 'The Archer of Charles IX!' why, Cavalier would be obliged to give a lecture on the history of France for every copy he sells in the provinces!"

"If you only knew the persons we have to deal with!" cried Cavalier.

"'The Saint Bartholomew' would be a better name," continued Fendant.

"'Catherine de Médicis,' or 'France under Charles IX.,' would be more like Walter Scott," said Cavalier.

*"Well, we can make up our minds when the work is
printed," said Fendant.*

*"Whatever you like," said Lucien, "provided the
name suits me."*

Honoré de Balzac, *Lost Illusions* (1837), translated by
Katharine Prescott Wormeley (1893)

How can an author tell when she is being "mulish" and "unlistening" about editorial suggestions (to quote from the Alan
Williams epigraph in the chapter "Publishing Partners") and
when she is simply standing up for her vision and protecting
the integrity of her work? How, on the other hand, does she
differentiate between an editor's genuine desire to make a
book or a story better and an editor's subtle egoism, philis-
tinism, or corporate toadying? With every book I turn in, I
like to believe I grow more adept at discerning editorial
motives. Regarding the skirmishes, I am proud of the
instances when I dug my heels in to defend my vision and I
rue the times when I compromised or caved.

In retrospect—emphasis on *retrospect*—some of these
editorial combats seem funny; others I have filed under
"valuable life lessons"; one of them I unreservedly regret.

WOODSTOCK, AUGUST 17, 1993

All was well, I thought. I had delivered the manuscript of *The Good Husband.* Hawkins had checked in. ("This is a big one. Compelling all the way to the end. Oh, and I'm relieved Alice and Francis didn't get together. I can't see them in bed.") Linda Grey had phoned. ("You brought it off! I'm going to reread it to get all the undersurface things and make some notes, but, Gail, the news is really good.") She said she'd like to drive up to Woodstock with Hawkins the following week and we'd go over the notes and make plans for publication in the fall of 1994.

In the interim, I went over the manuscript myself, imagining I was Linda. I improved some things and tried to foretell what she might still want me to put in.

They arrived promptly in her company-leased Lexus. When I went out to greet them, they radiated that nervous intimacy between two people who have been discussing the third in ways she doesn't know about yet. Robert fixed drinks, the four of us sat down, and Linda and John plunged wholeheartedly into trendy banter about some madam in the news called Heidi Fleiss. Then our fax machine in the next room beeped and started spitting out pages. "Oh," said Linda.

"That may be from ——— and ——— (Ballantine editors). I asked them to fax me their notes on *The Good Husband*."

Surprised that other editors were in on this, I went off to retrieve the notes and began skimming them as they burped hot from the machine.

The novel might work better if she took out that whole cruise section after Magda dies and had them stay in town and work things out there.

I'm sorry, but I want Alice and Francis to get together. I want to see them in each other's arms at the end of this novel!

There was more. Why was this coming now? Was it a last-minute assignment for the other editors? Had they just now finished reading the novel? Or had Linda known before today they hadn't loved it? Had she discussed it with John driving up in the car? Was this Linda's way of breaking it to me, having me read the bad news instead of her having to tell me?

Later, Robert and I would discuss what I did afterward. "It wasn't so bad," he said. "Your social side just shut down for a while. Under the circumstances, mine would have, too."

"What did I do?"

"You don't remember?"

"Yes, but I want to hear it from you. And please don't sugarcoat anything."

"I am not a sugarcoater, my dear. You came back into the room holding the faxes and told Linda you needed to be alone while you went over these notes, that you hadn't been expecting them. Then you gave John the big umbrella and told him to take Linda outside and show her the grounds. They seemed glad to go. You sat down at the big table and read the pages. Then it started raining harder and harder and I thought they should come in. You served lunch and told Linda you were going to read all the notes very carefully and then go through the book again and it might take several months. She and John said they didn't expect it to take you anywhere near that long, and you said you wanted to have the option anyway. Your chicken salad was excellent."

I packed up the manuscript and some yellow pads and Linda's notes, disregarding the others, and drove down to Asheville to lie low in my mother's condo and rethink the book. Her personality still inhabited its rooms. I lay in her big bed and looked out at her view of Elk Mountain and watched the light change. At five every day I went to St. Mary's Church for evensong. Father Edward, the rector, and I went to lunch at Grove Park Inn, and I confided I was planning a follow-up novel about Margaret of *Father Melancholy's Daughter*. Father Edward lived in the real-life rectory I had borrowed for that novel. He said some strangers had come asking to go upstairs and see the witch's closet in Margaret's room, but it was his bedroom and he had to say no. I spent time with my late brother Tommy's thirteen-year-old son, Justin, who had inherited his father's bizarre sense of humor.

OVERFRIENDLY WAITER: Now, tell me, are you two related?

JUSTIN: No, she's my wife's sister's girlfriend.

Sister Winters and I went on our usual picnic and brought each other up to date. She had been on her annual retreat with the Jesuits. ("My spiritual director said, 'Tell me about your prayer life this past year,' and I said, 'First I'll tell you about my life this past year and then my prayer life will make more sense.'") The Asheville convent was being sold, and the few nuns left would be moved to Boston.

Justin spent several nights with me at the condo and we went through Mother's nightstand, where she had kept her private books and writings. The diaries were with me in Woodstock by then, but her spiritual books were still stacked inside the chest, smelling faintly of her perfume. There was also her bound galley of *A Southern Family*, with pages earmarked. Squashed behind *The Cloud of Unknowing* we discovered a pocket-size spiral notebook with a day-by-day account of the time Justin had stayed with her and her husband after Tommy's death. The writing was legible though it required effort (this was before she took her calligraphy course), but Justin was ecstatic and asked if he could have the little notebook. "This is my *history*," he said. Later, after he had deciphered every last word: "Boy, was I loved."

I spent hours with my childhood friend Pat Verhulst, a college professor, whose 1979 story about her acrimonious beach trip with her newly widowed mother and sister had given me the impetus for *A Mother and Two Daughters*. ("Take it if it interests you," she had said at the time. "My nuclear family bores me to death.") Pat was the only one in Asheville I told about Linda and John's visit to Woodstock. She fumed with me when I got to the faxes and cackled maniacally at the big White Flower Farm umbrella moving back and forth, back and forth, outside the window while the rain poured down.

Returning to Woodstock two weeks later, less indignant and renewed, I revised the novel in forty days (lovely number), incorporating all of Linda's suggestions that didn't alter the book's structure. I found other things to improve; it is a rare manuscript that can't benefit from one more run-through. "Brava," said Linda and sent it off to copyediting. The cruise was left in and made indispensable by the lecture Hugo, the featured writer, gives to the passengers about beginnings, middles, and ends, in life and in novels. Francis and Alice remained friends.

IOWA CITY, 1969

Months went by while John Hawkins shopped around "The Sorrowful Mother," as the story was then called. Understandably the women's magazines balked at an ending where the mother makes a lot of food and then does herself in, but eventually he called to say that Gordon Lish over at *Esquire* loved the story if I would consider making a few changes. I said *Esquire* didn't seem to me the kind of magazine that would publish such a story, but John told me that Lish was turning things around over there. "More experimental stuff," said John. "People in the trade are calling him 'Captain Fiction.'" So I agreed to let Captain Fiction mark up the manuscript of "The Sorrowful Mother" and send it to me for my approval.

When it arrived, half of it was gone. "He took out all the dreams!" I complained to John. "The story doesn't make sense without the dreams."

"I'll get back to you," said John.

Lish told John the woman would be more inscrutable without the dreams.

I asked a professor on my doctoral committee for advice. "Look at it this way, Gail," he said, after he had read both versions. "A writer who had read Kafka might leave out the dreams, but it makes the character an entirely different woman. With the dreams, you pick up on her hatred; without them, she's simply an enigma. You might ask him to publish both versions. That would certainly be experimental."

"The Sorrowful Mother" was published as "A Sorrowful Woman"—without the dreams—in the August 1971 *Esquire*, one of the last of the elegant oversize-page issues under the distinctive reign of the editor Harold Hayes. The magazine cover featured a full-bodied portrait of a well-dressed gangster, all in sepia tones ("The Story of Joe Bonanno and His Son, by Gay Talese.") Beneath the title "A Sorrowful Woman," Lish had attached a boldface fairy-tale-like opening of his own:

Once upon a time there was a wife and mother one too many times . . .

WOODSTOCK, N.Y., 2014

If I type "Gail Godwin A Sorrowful Woman" into the Google box today, I find more fallout from that forty-five-year-old story than I want to explore. I haven't yet scrolled down the entries until they dissolve into gibberish, but most of them involve offers of essays to students who have been assigned to write on it. On one site, you can choose from a selection of free essays (pretty bad) or pay up to $34.95 for "better," "stronger," "powerful," "term papers," or "research papers." On the Internet the plight of the story's unnamed woman is examined from the points of view of clinical depression, suicide, family life, marriage, seasonal affective disorder, and first-wave feminism. It is "compared and contrasted" with "Briar Rose," "Bartleby the Scrivener," "The Story of a Year," "Barn Burning," and "The Yellow Wallpaper."

You can watch Paul Chi-Chan Yu's thirty-six-minute film of "A Sorrowful Woman," and there is a brief homework helper by David Wheeler, downloadable for $2.00 on Kindle, addressing the story's fairy-tale elements. "In many ways," Wheeler begins his essay, "this story is an inverted fairy tale—beginning with 'Once upon a time.'"

For a while I answered touching or intelligent pleas sent to my website. "I have done my best to deal with this text," a young man wrote. "Does she have a motive or is she just a sick, confused person? I don't want you to do my assignment for me, but any hint of what this story is supposed to mean would help."

I couldn't tell him what it was supposed to mean but told him how I wrote it and what had been cut out and suggested he just sink into the story like a warm bath. Take note of the objects and surroundings, observe how the characters respond. Don't feel you have to come up with a diagnosis out of the latest mental disorder manual.

When Raymond Carver's story collection *What We Talk About When We Talk About Love* was republished in 2009 under a new title, *Beginners*, with all Captain Fiction's cuts restored, John Hawkins phoned to ask if I still had that Lish spoof I had written. He thought it might be fun to send it to the *New York Times*. Back in 1969 in a fit of pique I had dashed off a story, in a letter to John, and then "excised" it, Lish-style. John couldn't find the letter and I hadn't made a copy. I told him I didn't even have a copy of the uncut "Sorrowful Mother," unless there was a mimeograph of it yellowing away in an old Writers' Workshop file.

GAIL GODWIN

WOODSTOCK, N.Y., LATE JANUARY 2009

John Hawkins phoned. "Jennifer Hershey called me again. Random House is still dead set against *The Red Nun* as a title."

"But I just got the cover art yesterday! There it was, *The Red Nun*, in big Gothic letters, and I thought, Good, that squabble is over."

"Apparently not. Jennifer has made a list of some other possible titles. She wants to go over them with you herself."

Jennifer prefaced her phone call with a respectful e-mail. She herself was okay with *The Red Nun*, but she didn't have any parochial school memories of nuns hitting her with rulers. Many people at the house, "including our president," were strongly against the present title. They felt it would put off many potential readers and hurt the sales of the book. I e-mailed back that the nuns in my novel weren't the ruler-hitting kind. I also reminded her that key elements of the story included a life-size red marble statue of a nun (and what the statue had come to symbolize to generations of girls) and a play put on every few years called *The Red Nun*, written by the headmistress when she was a schoolgirl.

The Red Nun was a novel I had been saving up to write for most of my life. When I was in my teens I wrote a story, "The

Accomplice," told from the viewpoint of a non-Catholic second grader who had just entered the convent school of "St. Catherine's."

> When she heard the familiar thudding walk on the dormitory halls late at night, when she saw the nun thundering across the wooden-floored assembly room to call roll before morning prayers, when she looked out the window and spied her crunching angrily through the helpless autumn leaves on the way back from the chapel, Nancy always went over the whole day in her mind and tried to think if she had done anything wrong.
>
> "The Accomplice," in *First Words: Earliest Writing from Favorite Contemporary Authors* (1993), edited by Paul Mandelbaum

"The accomplice" in this story is none other than Jesus on the cross, who is the only person the scary principal, Mother Blanche, fears and loves, according to the Catholic second graders who are giving Nancy a crash course in their religion. Fanning the flames of her predisposition for magical thinking, Nancy sleeps with a crucifix under her pillow and plots the nun's comeuppance.

St. Genevieve-of-the-Pines, the convent school in Asheville I attended from second through ninth grades, continued to allure and elude me from my twenties through my sixties. During those years, I began and abandoned many novels that might fit inside its haunting ambience. In 1987 it provided an educational background for the main characters in *A Southern Family*, and the final scene is set inside the rebuilt school, where the old nuns are praying for Theo on the anniversary of his death. And then, one morning in 2006, shortly after I had finished my Miami novel, *Queen of the Underworld*, I suddenly saw a whole complex story of girls and nuns that could fit inside those rooms and hallways that had been haunting me for fifty years. I photocopied a picture of the old Victorian building on a piece of red paper, put the title, *The Red Nun: A Tale of Unfinished Desires*, at the top, and taped this paper to the wall above my computer screen.

That gives you some background of how invested I was in the title *The Red Nun.* But I was curious to hear the alternative titles from Jennifer because, after all, Random House was my publisher and I had to believe they wanted the best and widest readership for this novel. She called and we went down the list of phrases she had picked from the book. None of them were striking or apt; she agreed she hadn't found the right one yet. What they were looking for, she said, was "something that evokes the most appealing aspects of the book, like female friendships and family."

St. Genevieve-of-the-Pines

"I photocopied a picture of the old Victorian building on a piece of red
paper, put the title, *The Red Nun: A Tale of Unfinished Desires*, at the
top, and taped this paper to the wall above my computer screen."

I reminded her that the book was equally about betrayals, female enemies, drunk fathers, and vicious mothers. And nuns.

Nevertheless, before we hung up, I had promised to "give it some thought." I tortured my brain, even resorting to the *I Ching*. This ancient Chinese oracle has never failed to expand my limited perspectives on any subject I bring to it, and occasionally it has stunned me with its uncanny prescience. This turned out to be one of those occasions.

Do not doubt your inner vision or ethics . . . Do not compromise your principles or alter your standards, for there is no end to the chaos and nothing reasonable can be resolved . . . Do not be tempted by promises of rewards or extravagant remunerations in return for your participation in a stagnant situation.

R. L. Wing, *The I Ching Workbook*,
Hexagram 12, "Stagnation"

Jennifer phoned again, and I told her I had given it the promised thought and concluded there was simply no title other than the one that was in my contract and already on the cover art. "For me it has always been *The Red Nun*, with its subtitle *A Tale of Unfinished Desires*."

"What about *Unfinished Desires*?" asked Jennifer. She was between a rock and a hard place. I could hear the strain in her voice.

That was my caving moment. I could have said, should have said, sorry, but *no*. But then I thought, If they hated the nun in the title that much, what if they simply withdrew all support from their marketing efforts if I insisted on keeping her? And after all, Random House–Ballantine had the license to all but three books on my backlist. I went into a cynical triage mode. At least I could save *part* of my title.

"Okay," I said. "Call it *Unfinished Desires*." I waited to hear the relief in her voice.

"Well, I have to run it past our president first," she said.

Later she called back. "Gina loves it," she told me.

I have since wondered what would have happened had I refused to give up *The Red Nun* as a title. There is a clause in all my contracts that gives the author final approval of the cover art ("within reason"), and with John Hawkins's help I probably could have forced the issue. But I didn't. It seems to me now that *The Red Nun* would have attracted more of the kind of readers who would have appreciated such a book. There are still thousands of them out there who went to school with nuns, many of them likely to eschew a title smacking of a bodice ripper.

On this subject of title mutilation, I have a further story from Robb Forman Dew, though it has a happier ending than mine. Anyone who reads Robb Dew's novels knows to expect the recurring instances in which good manners punish the inveterate practitioners of them. The titles she gives her books always perch above their ironic opposites, from her first novel, *Dale Loves Sophie to Death* (winner of the National Book Award for best first novel) to her recently completed family trilogy: *The Evidence Against Her, The Truth of the Matter*, and . . .

When her publisher asked that she change the last title of this trilogy to *In the Garden* ("although he hadn't read the book and there is absolutely nothing in it that involves a garden"), Robb stood up for her rights and threatened to withdraw the book. And so the title she chose was kept— with its cover art of a teacup and saucer of awfully nice china (the Desert Rose pattern by Franciscan).

Being Polite to Hitler, a novel by Robb Forman Dew.

But wait: what about my fight to keep *Father Melancholy's Daughter* as a title?

During the first year and a half of my writing that novel, my eighth, I called it *Vinca*. That is the title designated "Work #2" of that contract with Morrow. In the *Vinca* version, the reader first meets Margaret Gower when she is twenty-one and graduated from college. Her depressed father has finally gone under and is in an institution, and Margaret decides to use the first free time of her life to look into the circumstances of her mother's death. Her mother had run away with an old school friend, Madelyn Farley, when Margaret was six, and was killed soon after while the women were traveling abroad. But Margaret knows that Madelyn Farley lives at present in a town in upstate New York, tending (unwillingly) to her own crochety old father. Margaret goes to this town, gets work with a landscaping firm, and calls herself Vinca. It is her plan to work for Madelyn and get to know her and do some sleuthing. Then I reached chapter four and felt those familiar queasy signs of having taken a wrong turn. What to do? Time for a look backward? I took Margaret back to the age of six, the day she comes home and finds her mother gone "on a brief vacation" with Madelyn. And felt immediately in the right place, a child at home in the rectory with her depressed father. Their life together for the next fifteen years was exactly where I wanted to be.

Then I had to take a break and fly off to a writers' conference in Tennessee. On the second leg of the journey I found myself sitting behind Walker Percy on a small commuter plane. I was touched by how sad and vulnerable the back of his head looked. Melancholy, I thought: Father Melancholy. Father Melancholy's Daughter. Everything was in alignment when I had that title. And, two years later, when the new president of Morrow called John Hawkins and said of the finished manuscript: Look, John, *Father Melancholy's Daughter* "just doesn't shout big book," I was able to stand my ground.

WOODSTOCK, N.Y., SPRING 2009

Donna, the hygienist, walked with me to the window where patients paid for services. "I have to say it, Gail," she said, handing over my little bag of free dental products, "I'm really sad it's not going to be *The Red Nun*. When you first told me that title two years ago, I got very excited. It was the perfect title, it suggested so many things. How could you let it go? Well, meanwhile, keep up the good work."

She meant my Water-Piking and my flossing.

"You caved!" my brother Rebel had shouted over the phone. My sister-in-law, Caroline, who had gone to Estonia to get me a certain icon of a saint in a red nun's habit, was very sad when she heard I had let my red nun go.

At the end of the trade paperback edition of *Unfinished Desires*, instead of submitting to one more "author interview," I wrote "Some Questions and Comments for the Author from Four Characters in *Unfinished Desires*." These questions and comments can be read in their entirety in the Random House Reader's Circle edition.

I started with the headmistress, Mother Ravenel, the linchpin of the novel. "Now, Gail," she begins, "there were some things I liked about your novel and there were other things I definitely did not like."

I of course ask her what she did not like, and she proceeds to tell me. I got a thorough dressing-down. At the end she says, "Well, dear, let's not dwell on what is too late to change. But you weren't practicing holy daring, were you, Gail?"

Anyone who has read the novel will understand why that hurt most.

Onward and upward!

Flora, the Fourteenth Novel

A CHANGE OF HEART AND STYLE

There is a place in me I haven't gone yet.

Author's 2009 notes when starting *Flora*

Grandmother's storyline: This is what didn't happen. It's my cover up, and after I'm dead you won't know what I had to cover up.

Flora's storyline: This is what happened. It's all I know.

Author's 2010 notes while writing *Flora*

"You think this story is going to be about Helen," said Alexandra Pringle, my English publisher at Bloomsbury UK, "but when you reach the end you realize it's about Flora, and you are devastated." She was describing the reader's response, but she also was describing my experience of writing it.

I began the book thinking it was going to be all about Helen and how things turned out for Helen: the precocious and cunning child who became the accomplished and remorseful adult. But I also uncovered a new kind of character in Flora. Her story is over but I miss her and want her back.

"I thought I knew her intimately, I thought I knew everything there was to know about her," reflects Helen as she looks back over the summer that her cousin Flora took care of her, "but she has since become a profound study for me. . . . Styles have come and gone in storytelling, psychologizing, theologizing, but Flora keeps providing me with something as enigmatic as it is basic to life, as timeless as it is fresh."

Helen is ten and Flora, a first cousin of Helen's late mother, is twenty-two, during their summer together. Helen's grandmother Nonie, who has raised her, died in the spring, and Helen's father is off doing secret war work in Oak Ridge, Tennessee.

Flora was the first novel I kept to myself. During its three years of writing, I showed it to no one. At first my reasons for withholding it were practical ones. There was no longer someone living in the house to whom I could read chapters hot from the presses and have him first praise the successful things and then, in subsequent bearable increments, suggest where it fell short. ("Listen, I've been thinking: Margaret is eighteen years old. You have to give her a boyfriend.") My agent and first reader outside the house was slowly and painfully convalescing from a series of major surgeries. Also, I was not ready to make another contract: I was pretty sure I was going to seek a new publisher, and first wanted to get an idea of where the book was going.

But as the chapters accumulated and the characters' interactions pointed more and more inevitably toward the conclusion, the intimacy between me and this book became too precious to risk. Constructing this lean tale about the underpinnings of the self was more important than any book contract or suggestions from others.

Flora and I were alone together like ten-year-old Helen and her caretaking cousin Flora, isolated on top of their mountain in the summer of 1945.

"You have everything you need," I wrote to myself, "in this house with its peculiar history, the rutted road that leads to it, and the grandfather's cratered shortcut through the woods to town."

The seed for *Flora* lay buried in a 1969 journal from my graduate school days in Iowa City. I had just sent off the final draft of my first to be published novel, *The Perfectionists*, to David Segal at Harper & Row and, being hungry for success, had jumped straightaway into a new project.

"1000 Sunset Drive." That summer, when everything shifted and a young girl grew a carapace.

That house on top of the mountain! Children are like bombs that will one day go off.

One thousand Sunset Drive was an actual address. In the summer of 1948, my mother and new stepfather, recently demobilized from the army, rented some upstairs rooms in a house on top of Sunset Mountain in Asheville. There was a polio epidemic in town and I could play only with the children who lived in the house. Eugene was twelve, Jackie was nine, and I was eleven. Since we couldn't go off the mountain, a man from the drugstore delivered candy and comic books once a week. We would stand around the open trunk of his three-wheeled motorcycle and choose which comics we wanted. At the end of the summer, my family moved back into town and I returned to my girls' school run by nuns. I never saw Eugene or Jackie again and, soon after, the house on the mountain was torn down.

But that three-wheeled motorcycle would become the conveyance on which Finn, who calls himself "the deliverer," rides into Helen and Flora's isolation and becomes "the third wheel" of their fate.

I don't remember what "1000 Sunset Drive" was going to be about. What carapace had the girl grown? What had she done that was bomb-like? Within days after its single mention in the journal, I had begun another novel about citizens'

Three-wheeled motorcycle
On which Finn rides in and becomes "the third wheel" of their fate.

attacks on English universities in the 1400s. Nothing remains of it, either.

It was not until 2008, when I was helping Rob Neufeld edit volume two of *The Making of a Writer*, that I unearthed the mysterious 1969 lines about the house, the summer, and the bomb. The discovery was timely because I had been fantasizing about writing a novel about a young girl, isolated and threatened in some way. What measures would she take to protect herself, and what would the fall-out be?

Soon after I came across those lines in the journal, I read an interview with a film director who said that the mind of an adolescent was like a haunted house. A buzzer went off in my brain: "This way!"

Everyone quickens at the idea of a haunting, but if you are to make a success of this kind of story you have to find the level of haunting that you're comfortable with. There are many ways of being haunted. If you force your haunting story past the line your own belief can tolerate, the story dissolves in a puddle of fakery. I found myself halted by my toleration line every time I tried to force "the ghost" across the threshold of my novel. I was sure that it would be the grandmother Nonie's ghost and that, given her propensity for talk and instruction, she would manifest herself as an auditory ghost rather than a visible one. But eventually I let the voice simply be Helen's internalization of her grand-mother's advice, stories, and concealments.

The progress of a novel is never a simple point-to-point endeavor that can be traced in reverse like running your finger backwards over a road map. It's more like a pattern of clusters, with extensions exploding from the individual components that make up those clusters. If I hadn't eventu-ally scrapped the film director's temptation, *Flora* could have ended up as a ghost story. It might have been a good one. I would have tried to make it subtle and ambiguous, like, well, *The Turn of the Screw*, which became my secret model.

But here's the thing: I wouldn't have chosen *The Turn of the Screw* as my secret model if I hadn't been tempted toward a ghost story by the film director's remark. Both the ghost idea and *The Turn of the Screw* became my boosters, like the rockets that blast off with a space orbiter, then drop away. Only, my rockets stayed attached for quite a while.

James's novella was a dependable booster whenever my confidence sputtered. (Who's going to want to read about a little girl and her summer guardian isolated on a mountain in the past? Well, but, how many times have I reread the tale about that long-ago young governess isolated with her charges?) I even considered naming my little girl Flora, like the one in James's tale, but quickly revolted at the aggressive mimicry. Yet the lovely, old-fashioned name seemed just right for the simple-hearted young woman who would stay with Helen while the father was away.

The ghost story teaser, in the form of a preface, still clung to the electronic file of *Flora* I sent to the literary agency. In this preface people are sitting around a fire waiting out a storm and someone suggests telling ghost stories. One person says that the scariest ghost is the one inside yourself. Someone else ups the ante by positing a ghost that has lived inside you all your life and shaped your destiny, only you didn't realize you were inhabited by it until you were old.

"I'm wondering if you need that preface," said Moses Cardona, who had inherited me after John Hawkins, recovered at last from all his surgeries, dismayed us by his sudden death. "The minute Helen and Flora get together, I am hooked," said Moses. "What happens between *them* is haunting enough for me."

I decided Moses was right and deleted the preface.

From the start I had asked myself, "What does ten-year-old Helen make happen?" I knew Flora was going to fail or be harmed or defeated in some way. But I needed to observe them together, chapter by chapter: the artful little girl and the guileless Flora, who didn't seem to have any agenda other than doing her duty. What made a person simply guileless and brave? And Flora is brave, though Helen, many-layered and devious, decides right away that Flora is a

fool. Helen thinks she may have to cover up Flora's simplic-
ities and maybe end up having to take care of the person who
is supposed to be taking care of her.

Concentrating specifically on the interactions between
Helen and Flora, day after day, I realized that Flora was a
new kind of major character for me. Before now I hadn't
been all that interested in people who weren't cunning and
determined to win. Studying Flora, getting inside her enough
to figure out her responses (which were so often antithetical
to what mine would have been) became an adventure. It
opened more life to me. I saw for the first time the wonder
of people like this, people who live straight from the heart,
without thought of what is in it for them. They don't always
do well in this world, but it's refreshing to imagine there are
such people in it. Maybe the reader of such a character will
go through this process, too. ("Wait a minute, Flora's not
dumb, she's just modest; not a plotter, she's happiest and
easiest in acceptance mode. But she exasperates Helen. If I
were in Helen's place, would Flora exasperate me? Why?")

Flora doesn't have much confidence in herself, she tells
Helen, ad infinitum, but you can deduce from her stories
that she has been loved by the beleaguered people who
raised her; and two men so far have asked her to marry them.
The young soldier who delivers groceries on his three-
wheeled motorcycle to Flora and Helen on their quarantined

mountain (there has been an outbreak of polio) finds Flora warm and lovely, though Helen misinterprets his attraction as kindness toward a fool. Even Helen's snobbish and discriminating grandmother Honora ("Nonie") was disarmed in her last years by Flora's faithful letters filled with devotion and indiscreet confessions. ("Goodness, the poor girl thinks I am her diary!") During their six years of correspondence, Honora had encouraged Flora to make the most of her assets and to "act as if" she has the confidence she lacks. The older woman gives Flora pointers on how to present herself; she urges her to rely on courtesy and, when in doubt, to remember that "spoken word is slave; unspoken is master."

By the end of this novel I was surprised how sad I was to let Flora go. Having forced myself, in the character of young Helen, to coexist with an uncunning heart, I found myself, like the old Helen, mourning the loss of this person's brief presence in my life, even though I kept reminding myself that Flora was "only" a person I had invented.

During the writing of *Flora* I noticed that my writing style was undergoing a change. I was shaping a shorter, sharper sentence and working toward an essentialness in theme I found almost severe at times. Was I becoming harder to please or just losing more words? On days when the thesaurus fell short of my needs, I would snatch up the basic word, or the nearest that came to mind, and carry it to the giant dictionary across the room. It was becoming a necessary indulgence to *choose*. If the ideal choice continued to elude me, I would lug down a volume of the first edition of the Oxford English Dictionary, which John Hawkins had given me when he had his apartment remodeled, and sit with the heavy tome shedding red leather crumbles on my lap, browsing and sighing. An hour might go by. No problem: there was no deadline, no contract. Just my pursuit of the perfect match. Who would have guessed that the word *uncanny* had started off meaning "un-homelike"? No wonder Helen and Flora each felt the other's home life had been "strange"!

During the three years I was working on *Flora*, I also became aware that my methods of work were changing, along with my attitude toward "my career." I was in my midseventies now, having already gone past the life span of many of my favorite writers. I had outlived Henry James, who died at seventy-two, and before long I would be edging into Thomas Mann's territory when he was writing *Confessions of Felix Krull*, at the end of his seventies. That is not to say that I was becoming immune to the ups and downs of publication, the "picks and pans" of the business. A sharp enough "pan" could still send me to bed or on long, furious walks, and an unexpected "pick" could still shoot me into the stratosphere of too much elation (like that bus trip home after my first *Today* show in 1982, when I felt sure I had exceeded my limit of public exposure and was heading for a stroke). Even today, the "too much" highs, when they occur, make me feel less comfortable than the old familiar lows, when I can always buttress myself with the long-ago retort from the raven-haired tomboy in the 1967 Writers' Workshop, after her compeers finished trashing her story:

So? What do I risk? Obscurity?

During the composing of *Flora*, I found myself abandoning my computer screen and ergonomic kneeling stool and settling into the armchair across the room with a pen and notebook. This was a dramatic change. From the age of nine, I had typed my stories, hunt-and-peck style, the way my mother did. Her typewriter kept its place on the kitchen table as long as I lived in her house, and I was welcome to it whenever she wasn't clacking away. I had my own type-writer in college and didn't need one at the newspaper (though when I was transferred to a bureau and had to send stories over the Teletype, I did what Emma Gant did in *Queen of the Underworld*: painted the letters and numbers on the blank keys with silver nail polish). Until

Flora I had composed my first drafts on typewriters and later on computer keyboards. Handwriting was reserved for my journals and for correspondence requiring the personal touch.

But now I was opting for the armchair and its hassock and an array of notebooks, pens, and pencils. I discovered I liked the view from the armchair: my empty computer screen on its desk and a lineup of all my American hardcovers on the shelf above. It opened a new perspective on time. One day, like the millions of writers before me, I would leave behind an empty desk; however, I would also leave behind a row of books.

One of the notebooks was for musings and pep talks.

(Could I accept imagining myself into a manipulative child? I probably was one. Playing one person against the other. That first intimation that you are being used for someone else's purposes. Or that you are going to make use of someone for your purposes.)

(There have been characters like Flora. Elizabeth Bowen's Irene in *The Death of the Heart*: "Irene herself—knowing that nine out of ten things you do direct from the heart are the wrong thing, and that she was not capable of doing anything better—would not have dared to cross the threshold of this room.")

The empty desk
"I discovered I liked the view from the armchair: my
empty computer screen on its desk and a lineup of all
my American hardcovers on the shelf above."

The other notebooks were for writing out the novel the way authors had done for centuries.

> The guests, stranded by an autumn storm, were gathered around the fire. Someone said, "There's really nothing you can do about weather like this except wait it out. That's probably how ghost stories got started."
>
> "A fear you can control to take your mind off the fear you can't," suggested someone else after a wicked slash of lightning.
>
> Opening of the abandoned preface to Flora

Remembering Charlotte Brontë's handwritten notebook pages of *Jane Eyre* under glass at the British Library, I had to stop myself from writing the same page over and over until it was as pristine as Charlotte's. Even if all of her pages were as unflawed as the ones on display, I wasn't going to get very far if I allowed myself no crossouts. I enjoyed the sensuous glide of my Pilot rolling ball pen over the thick, creamy pages of the Levenger Notabilia notebooks. Covering the lines with black, slanted letters wet from the pen connected me with the flow of my whole life. The St. Genevieve nuns taught us to write using the old Palmer method, to which I later added flourishes and ornaments of my own. This method, which stresses shoulder and arm involvement, went out of fashion in the 1960s but is having a comeback as a teaching tool for those who have limited use of their fingers. It also helps prevent cramping. During my book tour for *Flora*, I would hear many parents and grandparents lament that state schools had dropped the teaching of cursive writing. Bill Griffith, the curator of Faulkner's house in Oxford, Mississippi, told me his nine-year-old son had been crushed: "But, Daddy," he protested, "I need to learn the secret writing."

Yes, there is something personal and meditative about "the secret writing." A slowing-down feeling of privacy and play.

But when does "play" turn into procrastination, like the old joke about the writer who has to sharpen all his pencils and polish all his shoes before he can begin to work?

"Well, you know what Casals said about play," a friend told me when I was wondering aloud whether my newfound "work habits" of leisurely penmanship and drawing and cutting out pictures of houses and people and three-wheeled motorcycles might not be dawdling—or worse, the beginning of senility.

"No, what did Casals say?"

"'The first twenty years you learn. The second twenty years you practice. The third twenty years you perform. And the fourth twenty years you play.'"

Performances

THE PUBLIC IMAGE

If I am an unknown man, and publish a wonderful book, it will make its way very slowly or not at all. If I, become a known man, publish that very same book, its praise will echo over both hemispheres. . . . You have to become famous before you can secure the attention which would give fame.

Jasper Milvain, the go-getter writer in George Gissing,
New Grub Street (1891)

Norman Mailer has evolved a theory that an author must create a public personality for himself in order to sell books.

Kirkus Reviews (review of *Advertisements for Myself*),
November 1, 1959

CORMAC MCCARTHY: This is a first for me.

OPRAH: Oh, yes? And why is that?

CORMAC MCCARTHY: I don't think it's good for your

head. You spend a lot of time thinking about how to write a book, you probably shouldn't be talking about it, you should be doing it.

McCarthy's first on-camera interview,
Oprah Winfrey Show, 2007

I. "BUILDING YOUR BRAND"

When my first novel, *The Perfectionists*, was published, in 1970, there was no photo of me on the jacket. Author photos were for stars like Hemingway, with his bare chest and white beard, and Camus, with his cigarette, and Mary McCarthy, with her dead-straight center part. During the course of the novel's production, nobody asked me for any kind of publicity photo, and I didn't expect to be asked. After publication, my agent, John Hawkins, phoned me in Iowa City to tell me that *Newsweek* planned to run a review of *The Perfectionists* and would be sending a photographer to take my picture. The photographer drove over from Cedar Rapids, shot many poses, but no photo or review ever appeared in *Newsweek*. "That happens all the time in the news weeklies," Hawkins consoled me. "They run out of space or you get bumped by a bigger story. Don't worry, something else will come along."

Soon after, *Saturday Review* (remember that excellent periodical, which reached its zenith in 1971 with a subscriber list of 660,000, and nosedived that same year when it was sold to the cofounders of *Psychology Today*?) notified Hawkins they were running a review and would like a picture if we could get one to them quickly, and so my writers' workshop friend Alys Chabot lent me her white cable-knit sweater, hurried me onto her porch, and achieved a very attractive portrait of me bathed in sunshine. The Jesuit president of Regis College saw the picture in his *Saturday Review* and was reminded of his late, beloved sister. Then he read the review, which compared me to Jane Austen and D. H. Lawrence, and invited me to come to Denver, all expenses paid, and talk to Regis students about writing.

That was my first author appearance, and though certain brazen elements of my performance make me writhe with shame today, I was treated royally and, some twenty-odd years later, was able to transfer those brazen elements to my character Magda Danvers in *The Good Husband* as she lectures to priests and seminarians about the creative process and does her best to shock them. This scene, from chapter two, is from the point of view of the young novice Francis Lake, who later becomes Magda's husband.

Though the lectern stood ready with its lamp switched on, she never so much as approached it. Instead she started stalking up and down the carpeted lounge. She carried not a single paper or notecard, delivering herself in a steady, confident, frequently amused tone. Once in a while she would slow down for a ruminative aside, or come to a full halt to scowl out of the window into the darkness, as if challenging the night to provide her with her next line. When pivoting around on one of her high spike heels for the return march, she would occasionally fix some member of the community with her insolent dark eyes. She was all in black: sweater, skirt, stockings, shoes. He wondered if she had done it out of deference to the black cassocks worn by the teachers and professed novices. But the sweater did not hide the curves of her figure, and she did not give the impression of being a person who did much out of deference.

Yes, I wore all black, too, and a huge silver cross, which I had bought in Mexico. When the president of the college came to pick me up at my motel room (which he had supplied with flowers, chocolates, and a bottle of Scotch), he said, "You are dressed like a nun." "Well," I said, "somebody has to keep up the old standards." Thus showing my ignorance: Jesuits don't necessarily wear clericals. Though one elegant old priest did.

He was to become my model for the august Father
Birkenshaw in *The Good Husband.* Here he is, listening to
Magda's riff on William Blake's plea to his wife for an open
marriage:

> Father Birkenshaw's high-boned face was a rock wall of
> cold courtesy.

My first book tour was in early 1982, when Viking Press
sent me on an extensive one to promote *A Mother and Two
Daughters*, my fifth novel. I found myself in front of tele-
vision cameras for the first time in my life. On the way to
the *Today* show, my Viking publicist, Juliet Annan, and I
took a wrong turn in the underground labyrinth of
Rockefeller Center and I remember us laughing wildly as
we ran and Juliet gasping in her low English voice, "Not to
worry, not to worry, I'll get you there," and she did. Time
stopped during those three minutes with Jane Pauley and
my face went numb, but I watched the tape later and saw
that a public Gail from somewhere sailed right through.
Several weeks before, *Today*'s Emily Boxer had done a
pre-interview with me over the telephone, so I knew what
was expected of me.

However this was not always the case on that tour. Thirty-
one years later, at the 2013 American Booksellers Association

Winter Institute in Kansas City, I offered up some book tour anecdotes at breakfast to Samantha Shannon, Bloomsbury's youngest, newest writer, who would be publishing *The Bone Season*, the first of her seven dystopian novels, three months after I published *Flora*. I told her about the morning TV show in Cleveland whose hostess, wearing a pink evening gown, informed me as soon as we were on the air: "Your publisher never sent me your book, dear, so you're going to have to tell us all about it."

Samantha, an early starter if there ever was one (age twenty-one, Oxford University graduate, an auction for movie rights), already had anecdotes of her own: while she was on a pre-book tour in Australia, an interviewer asked her how much her agent had made on her so far. "But that was easy," she said, "I simply told him I had no idea."

My book tour memories whirl around in my head like familiar old clothes in a see-through dryer. In the whirl I spot the awful things I did and the awful things that were done to me and shudder over them first. I remember strutting about on the carpet at Regis College and I remember getting up from a dinner table in Cincinnati, declaring in a huff I was canceling all my engagements for the next day, and stalking off to my hotel room. The local publicist knocked on my door through the night and there were flowers and notes outside in the morning, and of course I went through with

GAIL GODWIN

the interviews and the luncheon. What had set me off? The other author the locals were hosting had written a diet book and part of his act was to stand beside a life-size cardboard replica of himself as a fat man and give his spiel. At the previous night's dinner, the publicist had triumphantly informed him that he was booked on *all* the morning TV shows. "I'm sorry we couldn't get any TV for you," she said to me. "Novels are harder to book."

Though I'm sure I suffered as much as the publicist during that long-ago night (I lay on the floor and never got undressed), it seems funnier now, and quite prescient of things to come: that author in 1982, I don't remember his name or his book, was successfully "building his brand." All by himself he lugged his cumbersome double, folded to the size of a carry-on garment bag, on and off all those flights.

And I remember the escorts, those individuals who are paid to meet you at the airport, get you to all your interviews, and be your companions while you are in their towns. There are angel-companions, like the one in Madison, Wisconsin, who took one look at me when I staggered off the plane and said: "I am going to iron your clothes while you take a nap." And there was that prince of escorts, David Wenger, who founded one of the first escort companies in D.C. and would later become my model, even in physical appearance, for the character of Francis Lake in *The Good Husband.* Between *The Diane Rehm Show* and a bookstore signing, David and I were sitting in an outdoor mall. "How did you come to choose this line of work?" I asked. He thought for a minute and said, "It suits me to serve people's needs." This is what the young seminarian Francis Lake replies to Magda Danvers when he is driving her to the airport the morning after her strange lecture. (And Magda, being Magda, retorts: "What about your own needs? Who's going to serve them while you're off serving everybody else's?")

And then there were the devil escorts, like the woman who drove me at top speed along a Los Angeles freeway while regaling me with the details of two of her recent authors who had suffered heart attacks, one at the radio station toward which we were heading ("he vomited first . . . we thought maybe it was just something he ate") and one in this very car ("her tour had to be canceled, of course").

And there are the confiders who drain your empathy, like the young man who couldn't keep a girlfriend ("You've *got* to learn to play harder to get," I heard myself advising him as we pulled up outside a pharmacy to get me some cold medicine.) And there was the sad fellow who had charge of me for five days, up and down the Northern California coast: he wore a black suit and was enduring horrible domestic trials.

He wept inside the car until the windows fogged, and I kept reminding myself, Soon this will be over for you, Gail, but not for him.

And then there are the "compare-and-contrast" escorts, which are the most dispiriting of all. ("Sue Grafton always makes the bestseller list the first week of her tour. . . . What are you in now, your third?") ("Be glad you're not like X, she always draws a crowd, because people want to say they've seen her, but then nobody buys her book. Whereas your crowd is not big, but at least we sold fifteen books.") ("You're early! When I went to pick up Shirley MacLaine, her handler was standing outside her house giving me the finger. Shirley MacLaine goes *ballistic* when people are even one minute early.") ("I'm loving your novel, though I've only just started it. Last week, I had that writer who cut his own hand off, and our schedule was beyond frantic.")

At the beginning of my *Flora* book travels, in May of 2013, Bloomsbury arranged a brunch at Sarabeth's on Park Avenue South for me and my editor, Nancy Miller, and two other novelists, Caroline Leavitt and Emily St. John Mandel, who were also full-time bloggers. ("This is going to be smart women talking about writing and whatever else occurs," SallyAnne McCartin, my publicist, told me.)

Caroline Leavitt was about to begin a book tour for her tenth novel, and Emily St. John Mandel's third novel had been published the year before. I told them I was saving the final chapter of my *Publishing* book until I had completed my book tour and asked for their thoughts about the author as public presenter of her books. Caroline, who interviews writers on her *Carolineleavittville* blog (she had interviewed me in 2010 for *Unfinished Desires*) was just beginning a forty-city tour (with intermittent returns home for rest, she said) to promote *Is This Tomorrow*. Her publisher, Algonquin, encourages her to tour (on a budget), whereas Emily St. John Mandel told us she used the money from her French sales to send herself on an American tour and she was seeking a new publisher for her next book. Emily also accepted expense-paid invitations to go anywhere in the world and had recently returned from Writers' Week in Adelaide, Australia, where she had interviewed other authors and promoted her most recent novel, *The Lola Quartet*. I was equally impressed and alarmed by the amount of time both writers felt they had to spend on the road and zipping across continents to make themselves available to the public in service of their books.

And I was struck particularly that Emily, so generous with her own appearances and interviews, spoke with a respect bordering on awe for one writer at the Adelaide Writers'

Week because she would not allow any interviews. (It was **M. L. Stedman**, the London barrister and author of *The Light Between Oceans*.) This has stayed in my mind.

"Today an author has to brand herself," Caroline said when we were discussing wardrobes. Her trademark has become her red cowboy boots. This started some years earlier when she was invited to give a talk to 150 librarians. It was to be her first onstage appearance, and, being "pathologically shy," she asked an actor friend for help. The friend told her to prepare for the event as she would prepare "to be the kind of character who would be having a blast up there." Caroline bought a pair of ten-dollar red cowboy boots on eBay "because I was sure that a woman who would wear boots like that could only give a talk that would mesmerize. The astonishing thing to me is that it's worked so well that now people come to my readings in their own cowboy boots and want to take pictures of boots against boots."

I described my elegant silver jacket, bought for a book tour at an Emporio Armani in lower Manhattan twenty-four years earlier. For years I wore the jacket with a big Victorian brooch pinned on the right lapel, but for my 2013 tour, wanting to emphasize the "silver eminence" persona I felt I was growing into, I added a double row of silvery Venetian beads made by a Woodstock jeweler.

Emily said her main aim was to travel light, with lots of powdered soap to rinse out garments; but she had two favorite outfits she counted on—the identical dress in different colors. (Emily sews her own clothes, I found out from a later blog; I also learned from her blog that she has a new publisher.)

"By branding yourself," Caroline elucidated in a follow-up e-mail to me, "I also meant that readers want to be able to know who you are quickly—or feel they know who you are. I get a strong response from audiences whenever I say something personal about myself that relates to the book. For *Is This Tomorrow* I talked about growing up in the only Jewish family in a prejudiced Christian neighborhood and how I was bullied. This was so painful to me that I didn't want to talk about it, but I decided it was important to the book. A few books back I would never have revealed so much about myself to people whom I didn't know, but now I do, and I somehow find it liberating."

Caroline talked about the growing practice among book-seller-hosts of offering a "facilitator" to their authors, a local somebody or a fellow author who will engage you in conversation as part of the event. It takes some of the pressure off your performance, she said.

I found that to be true, but with caveats. It's a fact that audiences don't tolerate long readings anymore, and, unless you are a spellbinding reader, anything over fifteen minutes is long. Yet they want to see the author in action and come away feeling they know the person who wrote the book they are (perhaps) going to buy. They have gone to enough readings and watched enough talk shows to expect an *entertainment*. A facilitator can share the pressure, that is certainly true, but you have to be on the lookout for those who see their facilitating role as an opportunity to hog the spotlight.

I had two facilitators booked for me on my recent travels. After a few minutes of backstage discourse with the first one, an adroit self-promoter, I realized I had to set some limits.

"Here's what I've always felt most comfortable doing," I told her, taking refuge behind my silver eminence persona. "The bookstore owner introduces me and then I will come out to the lectern and read a little and talk about how I came to write this novel. After that *you* will come onstage and we'll sit down in those armchairs and have a dialogue about writing and then I'll take questions from the audience."

Since I knew and admired my second scheduled facilitator, the novelist Angela Davis-Gardner (this was for Quail Ridge Books in Raleigh, N.C.), I was sad for both of us when she fell on the day of my appearance and had to cancel. I knew she would have prepared scrupulously and imaginatively and that she was a favorite with local readers; the audience would be disappointed, too. So, after my introductory remarks about how *Flora* came to be written and the reading of three short passages from the novel, I said I was going to imagine the questions I thought Angela might have prepared and then try to answer them. This I did for about ten minutes. Then I encouraged questions from the audience "on any topic from writing habits, personal history, family, geography, psychology, religion, you name it." What followed was a high point in my experience of communal rapport. Not only did I find myself working out my next novel with them ("My late uncle was a judge here; I hope he won't mind if I turn him into a woman and move him across the state to the mountains") but a cousin I had never met announced himself from the back of the room. Then there were some delightful back-and-forths between me and a lady whose late father had rented my uncle his law offices in the 1930s, and between me and a reader of *Father Melancholy's Daughter* and *Evensong* who asked if my ideas about God had changed, "and, if so, how, exactly?" What was absent from that gathering was a single ego fluffed up like a hen on top of a rehearsed question meant to impress the room or challenge the author.

After the 1982 Viking tour for *A Mother and Two Daughters*, there were eight more, including the double coast-to-coast tour for *The Good Husband* that Linda Grey set up, herself accompanying me on the first one, for booksellers. I did modest tours for *Evensong* (1999) and *Heart* (2001), an East Coast tour for *Queen of the Underworld* (2006), where a reader commented while I was signing her books: "My, you've had a nice long run, haven't you?" For *Unfinished Desires* (2009) I did a New York reading at Barnes & Noble and was invited for a second time to the National Book Festival in Washington. In the spring of 2013 Bloomsbury sent me to seven cities for *Flora* (which included the January prepublication trip to the American Booksellers Association Winter Institute in Kansas City).

I often think about my return trip aboard the Adirondack Trailways bus to Woodstock after my first *Today* show appearance. On that bus full of strangers, I still felt too visible for my own good, even though nobody was noticing me. The facial numbness that had begun while I was talking to Jane Pauley had now localized itself in the right side of my mouth. This is the retribution for too much attention, I thought. I'm about to have a stroke. I was, after all, going on forty-five.

On the self-promotion comfort-level scale, I guess I am closer to the Cormac McCarthys than to the Norman Mailers and Jasper Milvains. (Oh, how Jasper would have loved blogging and tweeting!) Once I'm in front of an audience I can perform, but when it's over I collapse in solitude and wonder how I did it.

What make the performances worth it are the experiences I bring back and the connections and reconnections I make. I wouldn't have met the inspiration for the character of Francis Lake if I hadn't needed a D.C. escort for my appearances and interviews.

If I hadn't given that reading at the Ninety-second Street Y in Manhattan, I would not have looked up from signing books and seen Dorothea, my U.S. Travel Service colleague from the London days. "Please don't leave," I said. "I'm not leaving," she said, "I live quite near." From that moment until the end of her life, we developed the friendship we had begun in 1960s London. Dorothea had married a Harvard professor and was now widowed and raising her daughter, Katie. I would stay over at her Fifth Avenue apartment, one of those old layouts that included servants' quarters, and after we had talked into the night I would curl up between fresh sheets in the maid's tiny suite, complete with its own bathroom.

If I hadn't gone on a London book trip for *The Finishing School* in 1985, I would not have met up again with Irene Slade, the fiction-writing teacher from the City Literary Institute, who had set me on the path to Iowa with my English vicar story.

If I hadn't gone to Sweden in 1994 for *The Good Husband*, I would have missed that illuminating backseat conversation with my Swedish publisher, Solveig Nellinge of Trevi, after my talk at Uppsala University. We had been discussing Doris Lessing, whom Solveig proudly published, and I was saying how exceptional it was when an author—in this case, Lessing—had been able to access such a large amount of her material.

"She seems capable of using herself up before she's done," I wistfully observed.

"Yes," Solveig agreed. "With so many writers, you know, you feel their borders are never reached—not approached, even."

Even since the drive back from Uppsala I have been pondering Solveig's theory about a writer's borders. There is the vertical dimension to consider, too. You have to ask not only How far am I from reaching my borders? but How deep have I dug inside them?

II. REVIEWS

Some reviews of my book to hand. The qualities which people are the most willing to grant me are just the very ones I most detest.

-André Gide, *The Counterfeiters* (1927), translated by
Dorothy Bussy (1927)

That's Edouard, the novelist, writing in his journal. Over many rereadings of Gide's brilliant novel, I have tried to figure out what the detestable qualities were for Edouard. From reading Gide's journals I have come up with some guesses.

Book reviews and book reviewers don't require any appearances or performances from the author (unless, like Norman Mailer, you show up at newspaper offices to pick a fight with the book review editor—how many of those are left now?). But reviews definitely contribute to an author's public image. Sometimes even a well-intended review will corral a writer into a cramped enclosure she chafes to kick down. For example, "While X's characters will cut you up and eat you, Godwin's will bring you casseroles." I get which qualities the reviewer is trying to convey to her readers, I like those qualities, but please, spare me the casserole corral.

Toward the end of his life, John Updike said that he had come to believe his bad reviews and be suspicious of his good ones. That has resonated with me. I won't go so far as to say criticism makes me feel more comfortable than praise, but criticism has often made me stronger. Harvey Ginsberg, my editor for *A Southern Family* and *Father Melancholy's Daughter*, told me his rule for authors had always been "If a review makes you wish you had done something differently, file it away. If not, toss it."

At cocktail hour, Robert and I sometimes competed against each other in our Waves of Boredom game, which involved dredging up memorized quotes from our very worst reviews. The game's title derived from the lead of Robert's awful review, early in his career, in the *Boston Globe*: ("Waves of boredom swept over the audience when the opening notes of Robert Starer's Concerto . . .") Two of my big winners were "See Jane Think, See Jane Love" (*New York Times* headline for Anatole Broyard's put-down of *The Odd Woman*) and "Laughs Are Few in Iowa City" (Larry McMurtry trashing *The Odd Woman*).

Robert and I found Waves of Boredom so much fun, I think, because it reversed the stakes. If you wanted to win the game you had to prove you had been the bigger loser.

In Buddhist practice, negative and aggravating people and events count as your important life teachers. Some of my lowest hours, review-wise, have become my teachers.

LONDON, 1982

Robert and I are staying in the Primrose Hill house of my English publisher, Tom Rosenthal, who has planned a full day to celebrate the publication of *A Mother and Two Daughters*. We are to be driven to Cambridge for a booksellers' luncheon and then a special tour has been laid on to show us parts of the university not everybody gets to see. But when I come downstairs to breakfast, Tom reluctantly hands over the reviews in London's morning papers.

The four of us drive in silence to Cambridge. Editor Jane Turnbull at the wheel, Tom in the passenger seat, Robert and I in the back. Daffodils. Greening fields and hedgerows. Silence. Robert looks so sad. Tasty lunch with booksellers, one or two of whom make light remarks about the "silly" reviews. Robert and I are taken away by a lovely giant of a man in tweeds to look at Pepys's handwritten diaries.

End of English spring day.

A *Mother and Two Daughters* became a bestseller in England and Ireland. The devastating phrase applied to it on that lost Cambridge day, comparing the book to an American apple, big and shiny with no taste, never won a single Waves of Boredom competition.

WOODSTOCK, SEPTEMBER 1994

Late morning. Golden Notebook bookstore signing and reception for *The Good Husband* scheduled for midafternoon. Looking out the window, I see Robert slowly ascending the porch steps. He has been to collect the mail, and he looks very sad. The *New York Times Book Review*, to which I subscribe, is rolled up in his fist.

Another lost day.

"Gail Godwin is a good writer, but *The Good Husband* is not a good novel." That opening sentence won a single Waves of Boredom contest, I seem to recall, but more out of playful solidarity between the combatants than anything else.

And then there was the beautiful day in the Swiss mountains that I spoiled for Robert and me because the English bookstore down in St. Gallen did not have any of my books. (Hugo Henry, my prickly, embattled novelist in *The Good Husband*, throws a similar scene in St. Gallen and spoils a day of his honeymoon with Alice.)

But those ruined days now yield treasure, because Robert's sad face in the center of them brings back how much he loved me. "I am you," he said once, having rushed home from the city because I had broken a bone in my foot.

If another bite of a tasteless apple could restore that face in all its vividness of feeling for me, I'd gladly chew it up and swallow it any day.

III. THE PARTY

While waitressing and lifeguarding at a small hotel in the North Carolina mountains during the summer before my senior year at Chapel Hill, I kept company with a man who was certain I was going to become a successful writer. He said he could see it in my *Daily Tar Heel* columns, which were all I had to show at the time, and he could predict it by the intensity of my determination. He was a businessman, much sought after in his field, and I took his forecast seriously.

"It won't happen overnight," he said. "You'll get your start in journalism, then you'll write a novel and then another novel. And one day they'll throw you a big party."

We talked about this party during the several years we continued to see each other whenever we could arrange it. For relaxation, he liked to play golf by himself, and I would follow him around golf courses or ride with him in the cart. The party was to be high up in a skyscraper, the lights of New York spread out at our feet, everything achieved at last. We didn't populate the room; it was more like a stage set, waiting for its hour. The young Kathleen Krahenbuhl could have designed it well for one of her Playmakers productions.

On a spring afternoon in 1999, signing copies of *Evensong* at a bookstore in Hendersonville, N.C., I looked up and there he was. Much the same in appearance and demeanor, though he had been in his forties when we last met and now he was in his eighties.

"Remember golf?" he said, smiling.

After I had finished signing, we stood in a corner and talked. "You know, I never did have a publishing party to equal the one we made up," I said.

"Ah, that's too bad," he said. Then, getting into the spirit of forty years earlier, he added with a twinkle: "But how could anything equal that?"

Viking gave me a party at the Lotos Club to celebrate the publishing of *The Finishing School* in 1985. It was a splendid affair, held in the second-floor marble foyer with its Tiffany skylight and in the adjoining two-story paneled library with fires blazing in both fireplaces. But there was a bittersweet note, in that my editor, Alan Williams, was no longer at Viking (though he came to the party) and I knew I would probably be seeking a new publisher soon.

SATURDAY EVENING, MAY 18, 2013

WASHINGTON, D.C.

JIM AND KATE LEHRER'S HOUSE

The lamps are lit and the party has begun. First guests are circulating between library, porch, and living room. I'm sitting beside Father Edward on a hassock in the library, and Maria Bauer is on the sofa to my left. I have deep histories with both of these people and would welcome a whole evening alone with either of them. Father Edward was rector of St. Mary's Church in Asheville during the 1980s and '90s and was close to my mother until her death. He and I were close as well, and he heard my confessions once a year. He is all over my mother's journals, and appears as Father Devereaux in *A Southern Family*. On the next to last page of that novel, Lily is leaving the church after lighting a candle for Theo on the first anniversary of his death and sees the priest returning to the rectory.

> Young Father Devereaux was carrying a stack of neatly folded sheets and towels in from his little Japanese car. He had been to the Laundromat. They stopped and exchanged pleasantries. Poor Father Devereaux; it had not been an easy year for him. The wagging tongues of

The Lehrers' library

"The lamps are lit and the party has begun."

Our Lady's had taken their toll. Now he never had weekend guests at the rectory. He had gotten thinner and looked lonely and rather sad. Oh, the wagging tongues. If Jesus Christ had lived in Mountain City and invited His disciples for a weekend, thought Lily, indignant on behalf of the gentle and devout young Father Devereaux, who reminded her in some ways of her own Theo, the wagging tongues would probably have billed it as a gay orgy.

Father Edward has five copies of *Flora* for me to sign, and we sit together on the hassock and fill each other in on the last fifteen years. I had tracked Edward down via Google to invite him to this party, and he and his partner, John, also a priest, drove up from Baltimore.

Maria Bauer and I met at Byrdcliffe, the Woodstock arts colony, on a summer day in 1980. I had given a talk on fiction writing, and afterward an elegant woman came up and introduced herself, saying she had the advantage of knowing me a little through my novels. After retiring from the U.S. diplomatic service, she and her husband, Robert, summered in Woodstock. Maria had grown up in Prague; Robert had been a lawyer in Vienna. The two of them had escaped the Nazis, along with her parents, who had spent the rest of their lives in Woodstock. In our first conversation, I sensed that Maria was one of those rare humans who lives on several levels at once. She was socially at ease and cosmopolitan, yet I felt her constant radar scanning the inner vibrations of the people around us. As I was calculating how we might meet again, delighted masculine laughter erupted across the room. Her Robert and my Robert, both Austrians by birth, had been regaling each other with *Graf* Bobby jokes in Viennese dialect. *Graf* Bobby is a chuckleheaded Austrian count who, when you point out that he's wearing one black shoe and one brown one, excitedly confides: "And, you know, I have another pair exactly like them at home!"

The four of us did become friends. We shared candlelit dinners and swam in the Bauers' pool, Maria calling these our "swims parlando" because we talked as we swam, the three of them switching between English and French and German. I often wondered, swimming along in my one language, how well I would have fared if, as a young person, I had lost my country, my language, and my possessions and had to begin all over again in a foreign land. That is Maria's story in *Beyond the Chestnut Trees*, which Peter Mayer's father, Alfred, published at Overlook Press in 1984, and which was released as an e-book in 2012. Robert and I also visited the Bauers in Washington and got to know their son, Bob Bauer, who would later become President Obama's

White House counsel, and their hospitable, book-loving daughter, Virginia Ceaser, both of whom are present at this party tonight.

Robert Bauer died in 2003, two years after Robert Starer, but Maria and I recall when the four of us were here in the mid-1980s for the Lehrers' gala dinner to benefit PEN/ Faulkner. Robert and I performed a new piece we had collaborated on, "Anna Margarita's Will," for piano and soprano. (I spoke the lines.) Anna Margarita, still a relatively young woman, is fantasizing at sunset about how she will dispose of her worldly goods and gets caught up in imagining the lives of her beneficiaries and how they will receive her gifts. The piece was to become a favorite with sopranos because of its vocal adventurousness and range of moods. We had worried that we might have gone over the top with the humor, but when guests laughed unreservedly at the funny parts at our Lehrer performance, we knew we were okay. And at dinner that same night in the library where I am sitting now, the Canadian ambassador and I discovered our mutual fascination for that Victorian rare bird Wilkie Collins, whose "sensation novels," as they were called then, were the precursors of our detective fiction. The ambassador told me about a lesser-known Collins novel, *No Name*.

My sister-in-law Caroline Lee, whom Bloomsbury sent with me on the first half of my book tour, is rejoined tonight by my brother Rebel Cole, who has flown in from Chicago, where he teaches at DePaul University. Rebel of course knows Father Edward, having accompanied our mother to St. Mary's from an early age. Caroline has never met Maria Bauer, and the two of them have much to say, Maria with her diplomatic background and long residences as wife of the cultural attaché in Egypt, India, and Iran, and Caroline, who went to work for the State Department while still in high school and stayed on until she decided to risk a new career as a songwriter and librettist. Caroline has just seen a staged production in Chicago of the first act of her latest musical work, *The Last Storyteller*, based on her trip to Aleppo with my brother the year before that city fell. Chicago has a large Syrian population, and Caroline really did meet the old storyteller, who was training his grandson to replace him before the fighting began.

There are stacks of *Flora*s available on a corner table in the Lehrers' library. It looks good in stacks. A week earlier, when I was at the Bloomsbury offices signing first editions, my publisher, George Gibson (who has come down on the train for this party), took a sweeping photo of the conference table covered with stacks of *Flora*s for me to use as the screen saver on my iPhone. *Flora*'s jacket is one of the three handsomest of all my hardcovers, the other two contenders being the 1974 jacket of *The Odd Woman* with

Daniel Mafia's moody painting of a thinking woman in a wing chair and the 1987 jacket of A *Southern Family* with Honi Werner's painting of a casket spray of a single yellow chrysanthemum and two orange oak leaves against a branch of magnolia leaves, the whole surrounded by a vivid noonday blue. *Flora*'s jacket, designed by Patti Ratchford, is haunting, with its twilight greenyblue wash over the woman's partial profile, which captures her expectant, nonjudgmental attitude to whatever is in front of her. The title, which is her name, is raised in cursive white letters midpage, and my name, in upright red roman, is at the bottom.

"When I was in seminary," Father Edward had told other guests around the table when he was purchasing his books, "my spiritual director told me not to read theology. 'Read novels,' he said, and I have."

Earlier in the day, Paul, my escort and driver for the D.C. part of the trip, had said: "I'll just wait outside for you while you're at the party." "But why not go to the party?" I asked. "There are too many noteworthy people," he said. "I wouldn't know anyone." "Well, I wish you would come," I said. "I need a courtier." He did come, wearing a festive tie, and for the first hour of the party hovered in discreet attendance, bringing me one club soda with lemon after another. Then he spotted a welcoming face towering above the others and

his own face lit up. *"There's* someone I know. Donald
Graham. Will you excuse me?"

I first met Don Graham at a small dinner at the Lehrers'
when I had just begun writing *Queen of the Underworld.* "I
am going to put my old *Miami Herald* experiences in it, but
my young woman reporter is going to be pushier than I was,"
I told him. "And I have a character called Lou Norbright,
who is sort of based on Al Neuharth." "Oh!" he exclaimed
happily, "let me live to read this novel." He then entertained
us with a few stories of his own about Neuharth and himself
when Neuharth had been setting up *USA Today* in
Washington and Don was the publisher of his family's newspaper, the *Washington Post.* From then on, whenever I lost
faith in my newspaper novel, the memory of Donald
Graham's enthusiasm recharged me. "Yes, we bonded over
Al Neuharth," recalls Don tonight.

Now I'm standing at the entrance to the library, where
Jim has been welcoming the guests. I can greet Andrea
Mitchell again with a new appreciation for her work. The
last time we met, in 2006, we shared newspaper and
book-writing experiences, but until the 2008 elections I
wasn't much of a TV watcher beyond Turner Classic
Movies and *Masterpiece Mystery!.* Now I can tell her
how I have usually finished my work just in time to catch
her one o'clock news hour, and that I have come to

depend on her seasoned judgment and reportage of what she sees rather than what she wants to see. "I also look forward to what you are going to wear," I tell her. "You are part of my daily life." "She's part of mine, too," Alan Greenspan says.

Ron Charles, the *Washington Post* book editor, arrives with his wife, Dawn. He gave my work a generous introduction when I spoke at the 2010 National Book Festival. Then he dropped cross-legged to the ground (we were inside a tent) and set about tweeting the event. It was the first time I had witnessed someone engaged in this social sport. Ron Charles loved *Evensong*'s Margaret Bonner when he was still reviewing for the *Christian Science Monitor* in 1999; in equal measure he had hated Emma Gant when he reviewed *Queen of the Underworld* in 2006 for the *Post*; but he has given his wholehearted endorsement to *Flora* in 2013. We talk of his groundbreaking video reviews, which he says he makes gratis with the help of his family, and of a first novel by a young Washington writer, Anthony Marra's *A Constellation of Vital Phenomena*, which we both admired.

Now the party is fully astir, and Jim Lehrer clinks his glass and announces it is time for Kate's and my performance. "I want you two to stand between the library and the porch so people on both sides can hear you," Jim directs. Kate goes

GAIL GODWIN

first, speaking of the way writers help other writers and
recalling how, some years earlier, when she had stalled on a
book idea and was miserable, I suggested she write a sequel
novel about what happened to the little girl in *The Turn of
the Screw*. What kind of adult would she have become? How
would she remember the summer when her governess went
mad and killed her little brother?

Gail said, "You can call it *Flora*."
"But why don't *you* write it?" I asked her.
"It's not for me," Gail said, "but I would love to read it
and lots of other people would, too."

I remember being excited about this *Flora* that Kate was
going to write. I told her to read the diaries of Alice
James, Henry's invalid sister, to get a feel for the histori-
cal setting and in case the little girl in *Turn of the Screw*
would grow up to be damaged from the governess trauma.
On the other hand, the little girl might have crafted a
formidable adult persona to cover the wounds, and we
agreed that would be an even more interesting develop-
ment. In the end, Kate went back to her own characters
and eventually I wrote my own *Flora* about a threatened
little girl in 1945 and how she looks back on that regret-
table summer of her childhood.

Kate then turns to me and asks me to say something about *Flora*, and, while Jim is repeating his directions to address both rooms of people, I am blindsided by a rare bashfulness. I hear myself mumble that there is nothing more to be said, but Jim Lehrer, champion anchor and moderator, says: "Give us forty-eight seconds—and divide it equally between the rooms."

Somehow, Jim's "forty-eight seconds" summons me back to the public sphere, and I stand in the doorway between the library and the porch and pluck from the air some essentials about *Flora*. As I talk, I do a little dance step back and forth over the threshold, to emphasize that I am dividing my sentences fairly between the two audiences.

During the hours before her big party, Clarissa Dalloway lies on the sofa mentally defending herself against an old suitor who has returned from India and will be at her house that night.

> But suppose Peter said to her, "Yes, yes, but your parties—what's the sense of your parties?" all she could say was (and nobody could be expected to understand): "They're an offering"; which sounded horribly vague. . . . Here was So-and-So in South Kensington; someone up in Bayswater; and somebody else, say, in Mayfair. And she felt quite continuously a sense of their

The Lehrers' library and porch
"I do a little dance step back and forth over the threshold, to emphasize
that I am dividing my sentences fairly between the two audiences."

existence; . . . and she felt if only they could be brought
together; so she did it. And it was an offering; to combine,
to create; but to whom?

That's what I'm standing in the middle of tonight: a combi-
nation, a creation, something graciously offered in my honor
so that the people gathered here can collect, form new alli-
ances, refresh old ones. The living people I am closest to,
those whose existences continuously populate my imagination, even when I don't see them for years, and the
professionals who are currently sustaining me in my publishing life are all present in this room. Diane Rehm is being
appreciated by two longtime fans of her radio show, Father
Edward and Father John. My sister-in-law Caroline Lee
shares a love seat with my editor, Nancy Miller, who will take
over from Caroline as my travel companion in the morning.
Jim is calling his car service to get my publisher on the last
train back to Manhattan, though George Gibson is still insist-
ing he can perfectly well walk to the corner and hail a taxi to
the station.

Susan Shreve and I at last have a chance to be together.
We met in the late seventies at Bread Loaf when she was
always attached to little children and numerous carryalls.
Susan read a story there that I'll never forget, about an aloof
and faultfinding woman whose purse, when opened after

her death, turns out to be crammed with decades of clippings and cuttings about her daughter-in-law, who had always believed her husband's mother disliked her. In 1984, Susan's *Dreaming of Heroes* was the first novel to be published about a female Episcopal priest. The ordination of women had been approved only eight years before. Her novel's heroine, Jamie, made it less daunting for me to have Margaret, at the end of *Father Melancholy's Daughter*, seek ordination against her late father's wishes. Again in 2012, when I was writing the polio parts of *Flora*, I pored over Susan's 2007 memoir, *Warm Springs: Traces of a Childhood at FDR's Polio Haven*. Forerunners, inspirers, empowerers. As Kate was saying earlier: writers helping other writers.

Now Paul is driving us home from the party. My editor, Nancy Miller, and my agent, Moses Cardona, are with me in the backseat; Frances Halsband, who came down on an afternoon train, is in the front seat. We are pooling our impressions of the party.

Suddenly something out of the Arabian Nights—or fin de siècle France—blazes up ahead of us on Massachusetts Avenue.

"Look at that!" I cry. "What is it? An exotic embassy?"

"No," says Frances. "It's just the Cosmos Club, where I'm spending the night. It's much dowdier inside."

Nancy and I say good night in the lobby of the Hotel

Washington (now known as the W), where the rest of us are staying, including my brother and sister-in-law. Nancy and I will leave early in the morning for North Carolina. It's a good thing we can't see into the future, so we are spared the canceled flight in Charlotte, the perfect thunderstorm while she is driving us from Memphis to Oxford, Mississippi, the eight-hour delay going home.

Moses, always the gent, accompanies me to my room. Earlier he sent flowers, which we took on to the Lehrers' party. "If you're not too tired," I say, "come in and let's have a postmortem. The hotel left me a nice looking bottle of red wine and I'd be happy to see you drink it."

He opens the wine and takes the chair by the window, and I curl up on the bed. Of course we talk about John Hawkins first, and the last time the three of us were here in Washington, in the fall of 2001, September 8 and 9, to be exact, two days before the unimaginable events of 9/11. I had been invited to read at Laura Bush's inaugural National Book Festival, and had asked John to go with me to the reading and dinner at the Library of Congress and the White House breakfast the next morning. It was my first outing since Robert's death back in April. Moses made all the arrangements, including our reservations at the Willard, and announced at the last minute that he was coming with us, "not to the events, but to take care of you both."

We haven't quite swung into our party postmortem when there is a knock and in come Rebel and Caroline.

"Aha!" cries Caroline to Moses. "Now you have someone to share your wine with. I had my eye on that bottle earlier."

Rebel has his own libation in a paper cup and he has brought me a Meyer lemon for my future bottled waters and a small plastic knife, that item most precious to fliers. 'This lemon should last you the rest of your trip if you're careful," he says.

They snuggle up on either side of me in the bed, my baby brother, born when I was a senior in college, and his Lady Caroline, whom our mother would have thoroughly appreciated, had they been able to know each other.

"I asked Jim if you kept to the forty-eight seconds," Rebel reports. "He said you actually came in at forty-seven."

The lamps are lit and the party begins all over again.

Chronology

1902

Mrs. Craddock by the doctor Somerset Maugham, age twenty-eight, published in England by Heinemann after author agrees to remove shocking passages.

1912

Kathleen Krahenbuhl born in Selma, Alabama.

1918

"Proff" Frederick H. Koch arrives at UNC, Chapel Hill, to teach playwriting; Thomas Wolfe is in his class.

1929

Look Homeward, Angel by Thomas Wolfe, age twenty-nine, of Asheville, N.C., published by Scribner.

1934

Kathleen Krahenbuhl writes and performs in her Carolina Playmakers plays at Chapel Hill.

1937

Gail Godwin born in Bessemer, Alabama.

1942–1945

Kathleen Godwin works as general assignment reporter at the *Asheville Citizen-Times* and publishes under pen names in love story pulps.

1954

Confessions of Felix Krull: Confidence Man (The Early Years) by Thomas Mann, age seventy-nine, published by Knopf.

1957

Gail waits tables during summer at Mayview Manor, Blowing Rock, N.C.

1957–1959

Gail earns B.A. in journalism at UNC, Chapel Hill.

1959–1961

Gail works as general assignment reporter for the *Miami Herald.*

1961

Adrift in Soho, by Colin Wilson, age thirty, published by Gollancz.

1962–1966

Gail works for United States Travel Service in London.

1967–1971

Gail at University of Iowa; attends Iowa Writers' Workshop, earns M.A. and Ph.D. in English literature.

1968

John Hawkins sells *The Perfectionists* to David Segal at Harper & Row.

1970

The Perfectionists published when Gail is thirty-three. David Segal moves to Knopf as a senior editor, dies. Robert Gottlieb becomes Gail's editor.

1972

Gail on postdoctoral fellowship at University of Illinois, Champaign-Urbana. Knopf publishes *Glass People*. Gail begins *The Odd Woman*. Gail has summer residence at Yaddo artists' colony in Saratoga Springs, N.Y.; meets composer Robert Starer.

1973

Gail and Robert move to Stone Ridge, N.Y.

1974

Knopf publishes *The Odd Woman* (finalist for National Book Award).

1976

Knopf publishes *Dream Children* (stories); Gail and Robert move to Woodstock, N.Y.

1978

Knopf publishes *Violet Clay* (1979 finalist for National Book Award).

1982

A Mother and Two Daughters published by Viking (finalist for National Book Award).

1983

Viking publishes *Mr. Bedford and the Muses* (a novella and stories).

1985

Viking publishes *The Finishing School.*

1987

Morrow publishes *A Southern Family* (wins Janet Heidinger Kafka Prize and Thomas Wolfe Memorial Literary Award).

1989

Kathleen Cole dies in automobile crash.

1991

Morrow publishes *Father Melancholy's Daughter*

1994

Random House–Ballantine publishes *The Good Husband.*

1999

Random House–Ballantine publishes *Evensong.*

2001

Morrow publishes *Heart*; Robert dies.

2003

Random House–Ballantine publishes *Evenings at Five.*

2006

Random House publishes *Queen of the Underworld* and *The Making of a Writer, Volume One*, edited by Rob Neufeld.

2009

Random House publishes *Unfinished Desires.*

2011

Random House publishes *The Making of a Writer, Volume Two*. John Hawkins dies.

2013

Bloomsbury USA and Bloomsbury UK publish *Flora.*

List of Illustrations

Frontispiece

Louis Round Wilson Library, formerly the university library, now the home of the Southern Collection and Gail Godwin's archives.

6. Looking toward Bynum from the porch of Playmakers Theater

"I walked in my mother's own footsteps, until she would have turned left toward the Playmakers sunny temple, and continued on alone to gloomy Bynum."

10. Kathleen Krahenbuhl's set for Manhattan Twilight
"Proff said it looked very professional."

37. Anglo-Saxon banqueting hall
"Whether I was the warrior with the gold cup or Bede's little sparrow darting through the banqueting hall, we were all going to vanish."

45. *A scholar's reading room inside Wilson Library*
Where Gail's papers are archived today.

72. *Robert's Yamaha Grand*
"When Robert's health worsened . . . and he felt too sad to compose music, he decided to write a novel about an Austrian-born piano teacher."

83. *Villa Godstar*
Gail and Robert's Woodstock house.

85. *Kathleen's journals*
"Would you consider letting me put these in my Wilson Library archives at Chapel Hill?"

89. *Auction Day, 1990*
"It was raining, so we sat under the eaves of a little church on top of a mountain."

98. *Packing for book tour*
Silver jacket, Victorian brooch, and "silver eminence" beads.

106. *Grand Masonic Hall*
"I love it that the setting for this freemasonry among people of the book was the Grand Masonic Hall in New York on the night we were celebrating the life of my agent and confidant of forty-three years."

133. St. Genevieve-of-the-Pines
"I photocopied a picture of the old Victorian building on a piece of red paper, put the title, *The Red Nun: A Tale of Unfinished Desires*, at the top, and taped this paper to the wall above my computer screen."

144. Three-wheeled motorcycle
On which Finn rides in and becomes "the third wheel" of their fate.

153. The empty desk
"I discovered I liked the view from the armchair: my empty computer screen on its desk and a lineup of all my American hardcovers on the shelf above."

180. The Lehrers' library
"The lamps are lit and the party has begun."

190. The Lehrers' library and porch
"I do a little dance step back and forth over the threshold, to emphasize that I am dividing my sentences fairly between the two audiences."

Acknowledgments

Moses Cardona, Nancy Miller, and Evie Preston contributed immensely to *Publishing: A Writer's Memoir.* I am so glad to have them in my corner.

A Note on the Author

Gail Godwin is a three-time National Book Award finalist and bestselling author of fourteen critically acclaimed novels, including *Flora, Queen of the Underworld, The Good Husband, A Mother and Two Daughters, Father Melancholy's Daughter,* and *Evensong*; two story collections, *Dream Children* and *Mr. Bedford and the Muses*; and a nonfiction work, *Heart: A Personal Journey Through Its Myths and Meanings*. She is the author of *The Making of a Writer*, volumes one and two, edited by Rob Neufeld. She has received many awards, including a Guggenheim Fellowship, National Endowment for the Arts grants for both fiction and libretto writing, the Janet Heidinger Kafka prize, the Thomas Wolfe Award, and the Award in Literature from the American Academy of Arts and Letters.

She lives in Woodstock, New York. Visit her website at www.gailgodwin.com.

A Note on the Illustrator

Frances Halsband is a founding partner of Kliment Halsband Architects in New York City. The firm does master planning and design for schools and universities. They have received the Medal of Honor and the Architecture Firm Award from the American Institute of Architects. Frances has served as a commissioner of the New York City Landmarks Preservation Commission and as dean of the School of Architecture at Pratt Institute. She did the drawings for Gail Godwin's *Evenings at Five*. Her website is www.kliment-halsband.com.